BETWEEN CHARNWOOD
AND THE CHEVIN

ALSO BY BRENDA RAY

The Siren of Salamanca

Leaf Books 2008.

ISBN 978-1-905599-43-1

New edition 2017, published by Brenda Ray.

ISBN 978-1-527210-67-7

Gondwanaland

Circaidy Gregory 2013.

ISBN 978-1-90645189-9

e book

ISBN 978-1-906451-90-5

BETWEEN CHARNWOOD AND THE CHEVIN

BRENDA RAY

Matador
9 Priory Business Park,
Wistow Road, Kibworth Beauchamp,
Leicestershire, LE8 0RX
Tel: 0116 279 2299
Email: books@troubador.co.uk
Web: www.troubador.co.uk/matador
Twitter: @matadorbooks

ISBN 978 1838591 915

British Library Cataloguing in Publication Data.
A catalogue record for this book is available from the British Library.

Printed and bound in the UK by TJ International, Padstow, Cornwall
Typeset in 11pt Sabon MT by Troubador Publishing Ltd, Leicester, UK

Matador is an imprint of Troubador Publishing Ltd

For you all.

This is how it was.

Contents

Introduction

From the top of the road where I live now, on a clear day, you can see on the horizon, beyond the valley of the Trent, the blue hills of Charnwood Forest in Leicestershire. These are some of the oldest hills on earth; a thought which still gives me a thrill. From the bedroom window of my previous home, in winter when the leaves were off the trees, you could see in the far distance a big red hill. This was the Chevin, that long, low hill beside the Derwent, facing Belper in Derbyshire where I went to school, not showing the green of summer but the sandstone heart beneath, glowing in the winter sun. Close to where I lived as a child was tree-lined Vicarwood behind Kedleston Hall, and beyond, when it was about to rain, the Weaver Hills in North Staffordshire stood out against the sky. On the far side was the rising ground known to us as Jonty Farmers, between Allestree and Darley Abbey, where the University of Derby now stands. This, then, was the geography of my childhood.

ONE

Beginning at the Beginning

The first thing I remember was the iris. The irises grew beside my pram, which was in the garden by the path and a small cypress tree. I can't remember if the irises were purple or the yellow ones which we called 'flags', but the very first thing I remember is that I stretched out my hand and touched an iris. So irises have always been important. The shape, the texture, the scrolled and curled perfection of the iris. Under the pram was the dog, a gentleman among dogs, a small, rough-haired mongrel terrier who had been abandoned at a bus stop until my Land Girl mother took him home, the year before I was born.

The first actual *scene* I remember was looking out of a taxi window at pink lights shining on snow. I was with my mother in a taxi, going along Broadway in Derby to my grandparents' house on Stenson Road. She had just been to visit my dad in

1

hospital. It was Christmas Eve. Had I been allowed inside the hospital then, or, more probably, was I looked after by my other grandmother? I must have been very young at the time. For a long time I was puzzled by the memory of those pink lights, until I realised they would have been sodium lights which had only just been switched on. I think, perhaps, it would have been the terrible winter of 1946–47, when the snow was as high as the tops of the hedges near my father's mother's house. I would have been two years old.

Some years later, I remember walking along some endless hospital corridor to visit my father – yes, perhaps I *had* been before – and the horrid carbolic-soap red of the linoleum flooring which stuck to your feet with a squelching slurp as you walked along. Together with the equally horrid scent of carbolic soap itself, that particular colour, texture and smell will always be associated with my early memories of hospitals. Luckily, Dad didn't have any more spells in hospital for a long time. But he always claimed his torso was criss-crossed all over like a road map.

Having been (repeatedly) refused admission to the armed forces due to the illness which had floored him early in 1939, Dad had to remain a civilian during the War years much to his annoyance, as he wanted to join the RAF. He remained working on the railway, but became a member of the Home Guard, and I can still remember the sound of his army boots clomping up and down the garden path when he wore them for gardening. The Land Girl breeches and jacket hung up in the lobby for years, and were still in gardening use well into the 1950s. I often wondered what happened to the hat.

Our garden backed onto a piece of waste ground where there was an ancient and magical oak tree. Its branches were usually full of children, and our annual Guy Fawkes bonfire celebrations – very amateurish and decidedly wild – were held close by. I give fireworks a wide berth, even now. Another piece of spare ground came up to one side of our house; much more open, but also a fantastic playground for children. Our road was still unfinished, having been begun just before war broke out, and ran out of tarmac a third of the way up, thereafter consisting largely of gritty black clinker and large white stones. One side had a pavement. Ours didn't, though we did have a kerb. Weeds grew constantly among the clinker, until various householders pulled them up, and the gritty particles made interesting patterns under the skin of the knees when fallen upon, which became something of a trophy injury for us children, like a form of tribal rite. I still bear the scars to prove it.

The garden itself was magical, too. I remember it as being eternally summer, with flowering plants taller than myself. There were scarlet poppies with silken skirts, towering purple lupins that looked like knitting, crimson peonies with fat buds like babies' fists, tall blue delphiniums, and a scattering of bright red geums and orange montbretia. There were also currant bushes, both flowering and fruiting, with their wonderful scent. There must have been roses, too. Vaguely, I remember them as red and yellow ramblers. Most of them grew on a trellis on the far side of the garden, where I was reluctant to go because of our nutty neighbours. And at the far end, an apple tree. Later, Dad got me a swing. It was made from old railway sleepers. Like the plants, I can still smell them; an evocative mixture of tar and train smoke. The front garden, much shadier, had white syringa, which we called orange blossom, and, of course, a lilac tree. There must have been a fashion for them in the '30s and '40s, forever immortalising them in song.

Allestree, where I grew up just after the Second World War, was a growing suburb on the north side of Derby, where new development had begun mainly in the mid 1930s. It was a pleasant enough place, quite lush and leafy, and has grown enormously since then. Attitudes may have softened somewhat but on looking back now, it came over as an uneasy mixture of *The Stepford Wives* and Royston Vasey.

Most of the neighbours were to a lesser or greater degree eccentric, some possibly on the verge of barking mad. Or at least, so it seemed to me. My own family, not entirely exempt from cheerful nuttiness, were at least funny and friendly. Having been for a walk in Allestree Park recently, I was amused to note that the Allestree Frown, so prevalent then among the older women, still prevails. Some of the younger ones were pretty scary, too. The menfolk, seldom seen, tended to be greyish and crepuscular, rarely emerging in daylight. Perhaps it's just as well. Our neighbour in the adjoining half of our semi, tended to get up at the crack of dawn to chop down our flowering shrubs, and was one of the most malevolent people I've ever met. His wife, a thin, red-necked woman, was only slightly less malign. They had a fat, white, incontinent beagle called Bess, who barked day and night. She tended to wander along his rows of veg – he was a keen gardener – irrigating them as she went. "She sits among the cabbages and leeks," as Dad would remark, with a benign smile and a nod to Marie Lloyd. We often wondered whether they realised. Presumably they never needed to put vinegar on them.

One of the other gardens which edged onto ours belonged to a grim-faced widow who was a friend of our adjoining neighbours, and reputed to keep the ashes of her former husbands in two Chinese vases in her front window. She took great objection to my father propping his old bike against the fence at the end of the garden, and after dark every night, she would without fail come out and push it over. Eventually he got fed up with this and padlocked it to the fence, so that next time she pushed it over, the whole fence went with it. Which was tough, as Dad remarked, since it was *her* fence. But such were the niceties of Allestree life in the 1940s and '50s, that never a word was exchanged between them. This lady had a female friend, equally grim, and the pair of them, together with our neighbour's wife, would walk around the roads with their dogs, one of which flew at me one morning for no apparent reason as I walked to school, and bit me on the ankle. They were known to our family as The Three Witches.

More benevolent was Mrs Boot, who had a trio of dachshunds on a triple leash, which towed her along like a troika. She was a big, smiley woman with a smaller husband. Next to them lived a couple of chemists, husband and wife, who wore greasy raincoats and muttered suspiciously as you passed by; and on the corner, an engaging elderly couple and their middle-aged son who were tiny, dumpy and kind to children. They wore heavy clothing and boots, regardless of the season, went for long walks together, swaddled like Russian peasants, and were known secretly but affectionately as The Three Bears. They had a pretty bungalow with a landscaped garden.

Opposite us were family friends in whose otherwise ordinary bungalow I once saw a ghostly, skeletal apparition which scared the hell out of me. This eventually morphed into a short story I wrote, called *The Pin Man*. I always felt there was something inexplicably creepy about that house. They had a Persian cat called Ginger which ate anything that moved, then came to throw up on our front lawn, and two naughty daughters, one of whom used to sneak into our porch and eat our dog biscuits. It wasn't that she was deprived in any way. I think she just had a taste for Spillers Shapes. I was once terrified by a weird, whirring, rattling thing which flew at my head from that same porch, too large for an insect yet too small for a bird, which has puzzled me ever since. Someone suggested recently that it could have been a pair of mating dragonflies. I'm pretty sure it wasn't a bat. It was far too noisy and the draught it made practically scalped me. Alas, I may never know. However, the thought of a couple of dragonflies having it off is preferable to any more disturbing explanation.

Next to them were the Bottomleys, an elderly brother and sister. The sister was very sweet and well spoken, with bobbed white hair and a sort of storybook charm, and also kindly towards children, whom she would sometimes ask to run errands and then reward with a sweet, usually hidden in a very small tin which took her several minutes to find. I never found out if her brother was well spoken or not, since he never spoke. He was bone idle, with a long white beard, and was referred to by everyone as Old Joe. The only time my mother reported seeing him show any sign of animation whatsoever was one day when one of them set the kitchen on fire and he emerged from the house wringing his hands and wailing like King Lear. On the other side was Mr Brown, a small, delightful Scottish gentleman from Aberdeen, who later became a great friend; and next to him, Miss Clarke, a middle-aged eccentric schoolmistress and the world's worst driver, renowned for driving straight over a huge mountain of sand left by some builders without even noticing, much to Mum's delight.

Higher up the road, among the more interesting folk who lived there, was an actress, Judith, who worked mainly on radio. I think she was with the BBC Repertory Company. A friendly woman who arrived when I was at secondary-school age, I remember her being very generous when I was collecting for Oxfam. She and her husband bought the house previously occupied by the Quire family, whose son John was one of the few kids who had a bike. Looking back, this seems strange, as during the War years, bicycles were the most common form of transport, with petrol being in such short supply. Perhaps they had all simply been used till they fell apart. Also later came a ship's captain (why, in landlocked Derby, heaven knows) and his tiny, brisk wife, who produced a new infant with impressive regularity precisely nine months after every leave. She used to swear in a very ladylike voice, rather like a character in *The Navy Lark*, which was a popular radio comedy at the time, and they had a dog of impressive disobedience. The day they moved out again, according to my parents, the dog disappeared under the removal van just before it was about to leave, where it remained adamantly for several hours, to the tune of much high-pitched ladylike swearing and the joy of onlookers. Even the animals on our road were engagingly eccentric.

Under two of the small cypress trees in our garden was the jackdaw's shrine. The jackdaw belonged to a boy who lived higher up the road, and was semi-wild. It was very fond of children and used to visit me in the days before I went to school. It would strut along, looking over its shoulder, chattering away, as if to say, *Follow me, follow me!*, and would lead me to its treasure trove under the two cypresses where it kept small, carefully stacked piles of flower petals, all neatly sorted into type and colour, bits of broken glass, dolls' teaspoons and odd earrings that it had collected in the various gardens it visited. When the piles of petals got too big and fell over, it would clear them away and start again. The jackdaw had several different places for shrines, but under our cypress trees was the favourite. I will always have a soft spot for jackdaws.

The jackdaw and its collecting habits must have had a serious effect on me, since all my life I've been fascinated by small, brightly coloured objects. As well as bits of vintage jewellery and glass from charity shops, I also collect rocks, minerals and small fossils. I first came to look at fossils in the Peak District when my parents used to take me on excursion trains up into the hills and dales and show me the shells in the stone walls. They told me the land there had once been under the sea, and long afterwards, I could happily visualise the sea rushing up our little valley. I was once taken around the stone-cutting workshops at Hopton Wood, where every inch of limestone is crammed with fossils. Then, I discovered minerals – in a private collection belonging to an acquaintance in Ilkeston, then at Wollaton Hall near Nottingham – exquisite globules of what must have been agates, glowing like crystallised fruits, and haematite like compressed thunderclouds; pure magic. Years later, I picked up diamond-shaped crystals of calcite, and gleaming chunks of jackdaw-grey galena that I could feel burning my hand, among the spoil heaps of old lead workings around Wirksworth. But it was on a visit to Loughborough to see a colleague of my father's that the greatest revelation occurred. This friend, whose name I've long forgotten, took me to the window of his house and said, "You see that hill over there? Well, that used to be a volcano…"

I can only guess that the hill was the Beacon in Charnwood Forest, and soon learned that those hills contain some of the oldest rock on earth, and that the rocks of Bradgate Park, a little further south, are over 684 million years old. Thus began a love affair with geology and the earth that's stayed with me all my life. I can still walk to the top of the road where I live now, look out to the horizon, and on a clear day see the blue smudge of Charnwood Forest on the horizon and think, *Wow!*

Apart from the jackdaw and the dog, there was a bit of a shortage of playmates when I was growing up, since there were not many children of my own age around, except for a few boys, who were older and inclined to bully small girls. However, an interestingly unusual family moved into the semi-bungalow lower down and stayed for some years, providing me with material for several short stories, since they were engagingly different to the rest of our neighbours. They had two small white-blond boys, one of whom, Simon, was around my age, and the other younger, name now forgotten. They called their parents by their first names, Willow and Jackie.

Willow, appropriately named, was tall, slim and blonde, with a kind of casual sophistication. Jackie I can't remember much about, except that he had once been a racing driver, according to the children, and had a noisy sports car. They were enormous fun and their house had a large, airy kitchen full of wood and wicker furniture. The previous occupants had also been interesting, according to my mother, and had once invited my mum and dad to dinner, innocently displaying on their table a Dutch or German cheese with a rude name, which made my parents giggle. The only exotic foodstuff I remember the boys showing me was something called 'American sweets' (sweets were still on the ration here till I was about nine), which were enormous, round yellow things, the like of which I'd never seen before. I assume they must have been gobstoppers, but the only things I've ever seen since that resemble them are the large, round Indian sweets called 'laddoos', which are actually made of ground-up pulses and sugar rather than the boiled sweets we have. Sadly, I was never offered an 'American sweet', but I don't recall seeing the boys eating them either, so maybe they were for display purposes only! Disappointingly, this family left around the time I started school, so I never knew what happened to them.

When I was around six, a girl came to live in one of the houses which backed onto the side of our garden. Her name was Pauline, and she was being looked after, rather reluctantly, by relatives while her mother returned to college. She became my best friend and, for a year or more, we were inseparable, Pauline spending more time in our house than she did in theirs. This best friend was cruelly taken from me when her mother arrived suddenly, early one morning, and took her away. No one told me she was going. No one allowed us to say goodbye. Shortly before this, the family had adopted another girl, younger than us, and when I tried to enquire about Pauline, the door was slammed in my face. It left me with a sense of loss and rejection that stayed with me for a very long time.

On reflection, it's possible that Pauline may have lived in Derby for two years rather than one – but when you are only six, time and dates don't seem to mean very much. I really knew nothing about her, except that her mother, whom I never met, seemed to be a single parent, though whether widowed, divorced or not married at all, I never knew. I got the impression of indifference from both the unseen mother and the aunt and uncle to whom Pauline was farmed out. After they adopted a child of their own, the two younger girls (of dog-biscuit fame) with whom I sometimes played seemed to be groomed as special playmates for this child, and I was headed off with a shrill cry of "Oh, go and play with someone your own age" and the door was slammed in my face once more. When Pauline came to stay very briefly the following summer, it was clear she had been summoned as a temporary nursemaid and was not allowed out. Several times I saw her pale face as she tried to signal to me through the curtained window, but she was hastily ushered away.

For a long time, my life had a Pauline-shaped hole in it. Of course, now I was at school and there were other friends to be made, but Pauline, whose surname I never knew, had been special. After one brief, arranged meeting at a seaside resort near her home in Lincolnshire, when she seemed cowed and strange, I never saw her again.

TWO

Other Times, Other Places

I suppose I was very lucky to have parents who took me out to the countryside and to concerts and art galleries and theatres, which they did whenever they could. And although we didn't have a lot of money, with my father working on the railway, a free rail pass ensured that we had a seaside holiday most years and travelled quite a lot, mainly to the West Country where we discovered Devon and Cornwall, especially the Land's End Peninsula, when it was virtually tourist-free and unspoiled. We travelled on the old green buses, visited hidden coves and ancient sites, got lost on moors, and stood watching a lone fisherman placidly fishing from a small boat off Land's End one day, as six huge basking sharks swam around and under his boat, simply keeping him company. I was horrified, on going back years later with my own children, to learn people were now going on hunting expeditions to pursue or kill these gentle creatures. Hopefully, this barbaric activity has now been banned.

One thing I remember about these visits was that sometimes we would have to change trains in either Bristol or Plymouth, both still bearing the scars of heavy bombing in World War Two. I remember bomb sites in London, too, from the occasional visit, not usually enjoyed much; big holes, willowherb and broken buildings. Parts of Birmingham the train passed through on the way to the West Country presented a depressing sight, but it is Bristol that I remember most. Suddenly, on seeing that scene of devastation and brick dust, I got some kind of impression of how truly dreadful it must have been. Derby was very lucky to have escaped as lightly as it did. Even so, 'The War' hung about in the back of our minds as children, something not actually experienced, yet there. The War was a shadow, a murky presence. A word.

In the back of *my* mind, even as a small child, when people spoke about The War – which, in the case of my parents, was not particularly often – I used to think, *But there was* another *war. A war* before *that one. It was in another country. And I was there.* This 'other war' haunted me, along with certain objects – a celluloid fan, a red-and-black box of face powder with a particular perfume, a radio with an Art Deco grille – and words and memories that I could not explain or articulate and which puzzled me for a long time. Words, objects, snatches of music, certain colours, certain plants that I remember seeing on our visits to North Devon and Cornwall, made me think that there was *something*, something else, *somewhere* else, that pointed to a previous life in another place, and that place – and I began to talk about it when I was quite young – was Spain. There was no rational explanation for this, no connection that anyone knew about. It was something I kept mainly in my head. But it was there, and many years later, certain events, and in particular dreams, caused me to investigate further, and, after even more years, to write about it and visit those places and that time that haunted my dreams. In this strange way, the tragedy that was the Spanish Civil War has been with me all my life. All my life, I'd had the sense of not quite belonging. But that's another story...

*

I grew up in a time when food was still rationed. We wasted nothing. Sweets were rationed till I was nine. When they came off the ration, most of my generation went mad and ruined all our teeth. We didn't have fancy food, but Mum was a good cook and I never remember going hungry. Luckily, by the time I was born, the War itself was almost over, so I didn't suffer the deprivation of serious food shortages. Then when I was three, the National Health Service was set up. Unfortunately, I had rather iffy digestion, and acid fruit in particular made me very sick. I can still smell the terrible smell of the National Health orange juice, supposed to do us so much good, and instantly a wave of nausea comes over me! One of my earliest memories is seeing my freshly laundered sheets blowing on the line after my poor mother had washed them. This nausea, accompanied by violent headaches, was then known as acidosis, and later still, migraine. I dreaded being invited to parties because there was so much I wasn't supposed to eat, and other people's mothers could be horribly unsympathetic. I hated playing what I considered to be silly games as well, so any photos taken at children's parties usually showed a row of happy, smiling faces and one scowling little misery – me!

Very few photographs were actually taken during my early childhood, in fact, as I suppose film and cameras were scarce after the War. My grandfather still had a camera, and one of my uncles, who'd been to art college before the War, began to work at a camera shop, so most of the photos I have before schooldays would have been taken by one of them. One shows a back view of me and a friend called Sally Tabor, with 'wings' made of paper napkins pinned to our backs to look like fairies, and flowers in our hair, walking down our garden path. Sally was a very pretty girl who also appears in a couple of party photos, accompanied by a scowling me, and, like her mother and sister, she had beautiful, curly auburn hair. The Tabors were Londoners, as I recall, and the name is uncommon, possibly Jewish. Sadly, like so many people I knew then, they moved away after a few years. Derby in those days was always something of a transit camp, as there was so much work available, and continued to be so until the 1970s and '80s.

Another photo shows me, not scowling for once, with our dog, Ruffy, my friend Pauline, the new adoptee with her white-blonde hair and dark brows, and our dog-biscuit-eating friend, sitting on our back step, so this must have been taken before Pauline was expelled from our little world and returned to her mother. I think she may have lived in Boston, but I can't be sure. It all looked very sunny and happy, for the time being, at least. What happened to her? What kind of life did she have? I have often wondered. At least I have a few photos of those times. My husband's Hindu family, from East Bengal, forced to leave their home and country shortly after Partition, have nothing to remind them of their childhood. Nothing at all.

The dog-biscuit-eater had a younger sister, and between them, they were the most horrendously naughty children on the face of the earth. Our parents were the best of friends and spent most Saturday evenings together, chatting and playing cards for a few pennies while we children slept in whichever house they chose to meet in. We were then removed, grumpily, to our own beds when they went home. It was in their innocuous-looking suburban bungalow that I saw the terrifying ghostly image that scared me so much, and which I recounted in my story *The Pin Man*. Sixty-odd years later, I've no idea what I actually saw that night, but it frightened me to death and I never really wanted to sleep in that bedroom again. Like a child's drawing with a circle for a head, it stood and looked at me, then jumped up and down like a jack-in-a-box before I screamed and woke the entire household. To this day, I don't believe it was just a dream.

In their garden, at the back of the garage – and they were one of the few neighbours who had a car – was a large pile of tins of weird-looking orange-coloured stuff which I have never managed to identify. Whatever it was seemed to be dissolving in the tins, which were about the size of paint cans, and had the texture, smell and colour of pureed swede. What on earth was it? Some kind of polish? Whatever it was, it looked highly toxic, smelled very strange, and was clearly causing the tins themselves to actually dissolve. The tins were there for several years, as far as I remember, then suddenly one day they had gone – maybe the children had started to poke about in them. But I often wondered what that stuff was. I always felt slightly uneasy there, though it's hard to explain why. There were open fields at the back of the houses – what had been there before? Later, they were built on, but everywhere then had a disquieting air of impermanence.

Our own house, just across the road, had its spooky parts too, and sometimes I think I could draw a map of Allestree, and indeed of Derby itself, and mark out the areas of strangeness like isobars or something on a weather map. Interestingly enough, I only found out recently that one of the areas that tended to give me the creeps as a child has a geological fault running right underneath it. Which tells us something, I think.

I'm not necessarily trying to say that the areas where I felt (and still feel) uneasy were bad, but just different – *other*, you might say. Many were on sunken ground, like Markeaton, and Mackworth, where the fault line lies; but others, such as Bunkers Hill at Quarndon (good) and Alport Heights, near Wirksworth(bad)were high ground . Some, like Long Lane, or the path I used to walk to school, which linked up with it and was part of a Roman (and, probably pre-Roman) trackway, just gave off a deep sense of history. Sometimes, you just have to stop for a moment and look and listen, and the landscape will tell you what you need to know.

A cousin recently told me that there is indeed a geological fault line right in front of our grandmother's always creepy house at Stenson Road, also known as the Cavendish, and that something called 'a line of geopathic stress' runs underneath it. This is something recognised in dowsing technology, in which he is an expert, that can apparently cause 'an unfavourable reaction in the nervous system', so I am inclined to believe him. A few weeks after receiving his email about this, I read the report of a murder case in Derby which took place in a street just a short distance behind our grandmother's house. The killing seems to have been totally unprovoked and the killer was removed to a psychiatric unit, talking persistently about ley lines and magnetic fields.

On a cheerier note, the spare ground at the back of our house certainly had an element of mystery, with its ancient oak tree, gnarled and twisted, and circles of 'fairy rings' beneath. In those days I still believed in fairies and the little people, as many young children, especially country ones, did, and used to leave small gifts and food for them under the plants in our garden, and was occasionally rewarded with a tiny, handwritten note of thanks. I never found out which parent had written these, but believed in them implicitly for a long time. It must have been after I'd started school, as I remember reading them delightedly myself. I also remember convincing myself that I had heard two cats speaking to each other in human voices under that same oak tree.

When I was a bit older, and past the belief-in-fairies stage, I had a very imaginative friend called Margaret, with whom I invented a sort of gremlin figure called The Little Brown Man. If anyone has ever heard the story of the allegedly haunted Lincoln bomber which is now in the RAF Museum at Cosford – it's a modified Lancaster, if anyone's feeling pedantic – they will recognise the elements of this story. But it's true. The Little Brown Man we invented was responsible for anything we lost. If anything disappeared, The Little Brown Man had taken it. The Little Brown Man lived in the coalhouse (which may have been the site of the buzzing, whirring thing described earlier, rather than the porch – memory defeats me here), which was a dark, dank place attached to the house and backing up to the pantry, also dark and rather cold. One day, my school beret was missing. This was a punishable offence. I grew up in a time of violent teachers. Half of them had just left the army. We searched and searched to no avail. No one was home except us. We searched the garden, the street outside, ransacked the house. Clearly, The Little Brown Man had been at work again. Eventually, there was nothing else for it. Cautiously, we opened the coalhouse door and peered inside. In the dark recesses, something moved! Horrified, we fled, shrieking, to the top of the road as fast as our legs could carry us. It was a very long time before I went near the coalhouse again, if ever, as we moved house not long afterwards. And the beret? Weirdly enough, shortly after I plucked up courage to go back in the house, it reappeared, neatly hooked over a bottle of lemonade in the pantry, where we'd looked moments before... Which, like the Lincoln bomber gremlin, goes to show that if you make up a story and persuade people hard enough that it's true, then one day, it will be!

*

Not long after the event of The Little Brown Man, my parents moved to a bungalow across the road, next to the allegedly haunted one. Strangely enough, although it did seem a bit alien at first, I never felt particularly uneasy in this house, though I remember Margaret saying, "Maybe you'll have a Little Green Man in there, instead!" I didn't take her up on that one. However, some years before this, the wild area at the back of the house had been built on, and the magical oak tree cut down, to everyone's great distress. All our childhood play areas were beginning to disappear. Nonetheless, even though new housing estates were beginning to spring up, that air of impermanence was to last a good deal longer.

At the top of the road, a rough track petered away into nothing, but had kerbstones laid out for some distance on either side, presumably begun before the outbreak of war in 1939. Our own road simply stopped at the top end, where it faded into fields. Across the top of the first field, an ancient trackway led towards Allestree Lane in one direction and Quarn Turn in the other, passing down what we called Hunter's Ditch, a deep and delightfully creepy scooped-out footpath that my grandmother, who was born not far away, simply called The Hollow. My mother told me it was part of a Roman road that led from Little Chester on the far side of the Derwent to the salt fields near Nantwich in Cheshire, and much of it can still be followed today, as it crosses Kedleston and Mackworth and leads onto Long Lane, which does indeed head across that way. Long Lane itself is engagingly eerie, and, being so long and straight and seemingly endless when you drive along it, can be surprisingly hypnotic. At one point, it follows exactly line of latitude 38 for a distance of several miles. Sometimes bare and exposed, and in one part shadowed and enclosed in a deep hollow, it never fails to fascinate.

Many people have reported strange figures and odd jumps in time along Long Lane, and so have I. But this came later, as when I was a child we had no car so Long Lane, then, was undiscovered territory. But yes, I did see something. Not Roman soldiers, as some people have reported, or Victorian farmworkers, but medieval people – poor people; men, women and children – walking endlessly along Long Lane up the gradual slope towards Alkmonton, carrying staffs and bundles, with their dogs running beside them. It was late in the 1960s when I first became aware of them. I had recently married, and we had a car, and, driving along the endless, ancient road, suddenly, there they were, always in front of us, both there and not there. People, I concluded, from one of those deserted medieval villages along the Lane, of which there are several. Always a little in front of us, we never drove through them or caught up with them. Many times I saw them, then one day they were gone and I could never glimpse them again.[1]

---

1   The story *The Pin Man* can be found in *The Siren of Salamanca*, together with several other stories of a supernatural nature.

THREE

Several Weddings and a Funeral

As I mentioned before, there are not many photos from my childhood. There is one of my mother, my grandmother and me standing at the entrance to The Hollow, or Hunter's Ditch, taken when I was very small; and another at Twyford around the same time. These would have been taken by my grandfather, who at one time used to develop and print his own pictures in a makeshift darkroom under the stairs at their home in Stenson Road. Twyford was a place where they went to picnic and became friendly with the lady who operated the ferry across the River Trent; a strange, flat-bottomed, chain-driven craft that would take a small herd of cattle from the grazing on one side of the river to the other. Her name was Mabel, and I remember her well. My youngest uncle, who had given up his place at art college to serve in the Fleet Air Arm, visited her occasionally long after my grandparents had passed away, and when he died in the 1980s, a strange old woman in black whom nobody could identify appeared at the funeral. She identified herself as Mabel, 'Mabel from the ferry' from all those years before, and I remember another uncle saying he had given her some money for a taxi home. The totally unexpected appearance of a ferrywoman at a funeral seemed strangely significant, for, indeed, who pays the ferryman?

The uncle who visited the ferrywoman became the family photographer to a certain extent, and worked in a camera shop for some years after he left the services. When he married, I was one of his bridesmaids, and I remember going with his wife-to-be to try on my bridesmaid's dress somewhere in town. She took me for tea at the cafe in the Picture House, one of the town's oldest and quirkiest cinemas, which was allegedly based on the Minstrels' Gallery in Haddon Hall, and I can recall hearing music and laughter from a film called *Tea for Two* playing in the cinema. I checked to ascertain the year, and it was released in 1950, so I would have been six. The year I met Pauline, which adds up pretty well with my memories. Weirdly enough, I can't remember trying on the dress at all, but I suppose tea and toasted teacakes are a lot more important when you're six. There were several high-class dress shops in Babington Lane, where the cinema was – Brindleys, opposite, and higher up, Bracegirdles, almost too posh to go into, though the name itself seemed to imply bolster-shaped ladies in hook-sided corsets. That particular shop is still a ladies' outfitters today, but the Picture House Cinema, originally the Midland Electric Theatre, was unforgivably demolished in the late 1960s and the site became Derby's first Primark store, a tatty-looking building from Day One, and now a charity furniture store. Much as I love Primark and second-hand bookcases (and I do, I do!),

I'd rather it was still a lovely little 1910 cinema with a quaint cafe and a barrel-vaulted ceiling!

There are a few photos of me at that wedding, in my little white puff-sleeved dress; then the following Easter, my other uncle (my mother's younger brother, who'd been married once before, briefly and unhappily, during the War) married again, and I wore the same dress to his wedding. This time, the photographs show a slightly older and rather unhappy-looking child, shivering in the cold, a velvet cloak partially covering the dress. It was a bitter day, and I caught a chill which developed into pneumonia, rapidly becoming too ill to go home, and spent a long time in my grandmother's front bedroom, being dosed with horrendous things called M&B tablets, which were about the size of half-crowns. These were unsuccessfully 'disguised' in a spoonful of raspberry jam, and I spent many nights trying to sleep in my grandma's big bed in the front room at Stenson Road, watching the lights of cars carve across the window and ceiling as they came down Warwick Avenue and round the traffic island at the bottom. (Or occasionally not, as it was something of an accident black spot. On one occasion, an entire lorry load of lavatories overturned right outside Grandma's front gate.) I recovered from the pneumonia by the skin of my teeth and was eventually taken by my mother and grandmother to Skegness for a week to recuperate. The only thing that kept me awake in the night there was the sound of lions roaring – there was a circus billeted nearby!

The next family wedding was on my dad's side; that of my oldest cousin, a one-time librarian, twelve years older than me, who married a local farmer. I was not asked to be a bridesmaid on this occasion – perhaps nobody wanted to tempt fate again – and, as the wedding must have been on a school day, didn't go to it either. All I can remember is my mother bringing me some food back, then forgetting it after she'd left it in the oven to warm up and burning it to a cinder, while she was chatting to a neighbour. I was livid! This neighbour would have been Pauline's aunt and I suspect this must have been before she left, after which relations cooled somewhat. Another occasion I remember Mum talking to this neighbour, with whom she was not especially friendly, would have been in 1952, a day when we switched on the radio and nothing happened. My mother concluded that the King (George VI) must have died – she went outside to find someone to ask, and it was confirmed that this was the case. I have recently read that the announcement was not made until 10.45am, and the BBC closed down for the rest of the day after informing the nation at 11.15, except for the occasional special announcement, so I could not have been at school that Wednesday morning, 6th February 1952.

My cousin's new husband the farmer was quite a character, and used to drive a Land Rover, or more probably a recycled ex-army jeep, which he would back down our road at horrendous speed, much to our amusement, since at the time the road ended at the top in a pile of shale and clinker before degenerating into fields which would eventually be built on once the rest of the road was completed. After that, there didn't seem to be any more weddings till around 1960, as on one side of the family, Dad was the youngest and his brothers' children were much older than me, while on the other, with Mum being the eldest, everyone was much younger, so there was a lack of relatives of a suitable age for marriage, or of the same age as myself. The only cousin roughly my age was born a couple of years earlier in Cornwall and his parents had separated before the War ended. His grandmother and mine stayed in touch and I occasionally saw photos of him, but we never met until his stepmother (at whose wedding I caught pneumonia!) died, by which time we were both in our sixties. We met at her funeral along with other family members, and found we had a great deal in common and have been in touch ever since. Like me, he studies the paranormal as well as family history, and has written books on ley lines and dowsing. Now, at last, we can compare notes.

I had one cousin to whom I was quite close, eight years older than me to the day, with whom I used to go out on slightly mad escapades from time to time. She, too, was a child of a broken wartime marriage, this one involving considerable scandal, unfortunately, and eventually she and her younger brother were found places at boarding schools, since their father, to whom custody had been granted, had difficulty looking after them while he was at work all day. Tessa was a good companion, and I missed her, but of course, the age gap between us was so wide that she was more like an aunt than a cousin. Eventually she married a Greek doctor and spent much time abroad, so I rarely saw her. The marriage did not seem to have been very happy, and they, too, separated, and sadly, she died quite young.

One of the places that Tessa and I explored in the days before I went to school was Markeaton Park. At this time, the house (Markeaton Hall) was still standing, a gloomy and semi-derelict pile which had been badly trashed by troops during the War. There was also a partially burned cottage in the grounds near the old village side (the thatch had caught fire, I think), which we found interesting, and I remember being shouted at for swinging on one of the low-growing trees just outside it. I still find the area around Markeaton eerie to this day. I often seemed to get shouted at when I went out with Tess. Can't think why…

Markeaton had once been a much bigger village, but now consists of only a scattered cottage or two, one of which is a garden centre, and of course the park, which presumably overtook the rest of the village, although it always seems to have shared a church with Mackworth, across the fields. Mackworth, too, was once much larger, although the story of its castle may well have been something of a myth. There is, however, an impressive stone gateway to a farmhouse, which is said to have been its entrance. The old story was that Oliver Cromwell (who, along with Henry VIII, got the blame for everything) and his troops had a cannon close to the rising ground by my great-grandfather's cottage in Quarndon and blew it down. It's still called Cannon Hill to this day. There's a 1950s Hollywood costume drama, starring Tony Curtis as some rather improbable English knight, called *The Black Shield of Falworth*, some of which, weirdly enough, is set at Mackworth Castle. My husband was a sucker for this kind of movie, which we used to watch together on TV, and it always made us laugh and wonder how they picked the name. Maybe some technician on the set, realising they had no name for the place, said, "I used to live at a place called Mackworth in England, which had a castle...", and so that was what they chose. I have an old watercolour, unlabelled and undated, which appears to show one of the cottages, since much altered, on Markeaton Lane, close to where the footpath leads to Mackworth Church. Almost opposite, towards the Ashbourne Road, a crematorium was built in the mid 1950s, somewhat spoiling its original charm.

Another of our haunts was around Markeaton Brook and the small potholed tracks that led down to it, where there were prefabs and shacks off Kedleston Road with what seemed to me very strange names – Menin Road, Somme Road, Ypres and Lens Roads etc. I was puzzled by these as a child and later learned that ex-soldiers from the First World War had been allowed to have allotments and build shacks there. Although strictly speaking they were not supposed to live in them, of course they did, and in later years, the prefabs sprang up too. There were some pretty rough characters living there who would yell at us to go away, which we found very exciting. I have to laugh now when I see the luxury homes that have been built in their place and wonder if the residents have any idea what it was like before! There were a few prefabs and old army huts in Markeaton Park, too, which were still occupied then. I had wondered until recently if I had imagined this, until some letters to the *Derby Telegraph* confirmed that the huts in the park had been occupied by people waiting for council houses which had been promised before the War, and that several correspondents remembered living in them.

Another place Tess and I used to go was known locally as Jonty Farmers. This was the area of land roughly where Park Farm Shopping Centre and the university stand today, and not where the modern pub called the Jonty Farmer is at all. Jonty Farmers was high up on the hill, and the reason we liked it was because there were usually horses there. We were both fond of horses and Tess could ride a bit, as did I for a while when I was ten or so, until the cost went up from five shillings to ten shillings an hour and I could no longer afford it. In front of where the university now stands had originally been Markeaton Golf Course, and it was eventually built on, becoming Birchover Way and the Park Farm Shopping Centre. The college was built and opened around 1960. Walking from where we lived, you could go over Jonty Farmers and come down towards the part of Kedleston Road near to the Markeaton Hotel where my other grandmother, my dad's mother, lived. An elderly man who used to sweep chimneys around Allestree told my mother that he used to train horses for the Derbyshire Yeomanry up there in years gone by.

The sweeps and blacksmiths were real characters who seemed to be part of a vanished world. This elderly chimney sweep was called Mr Summers, from Darley Abbey, and he used to ride around on an ancient motorbike in a cloud of black dust. He was not our original sweep, who was the Quarndon one, Mr Heathcote, pronounced to rhyme with 'breath-cut' and minus the first 'H'. Mr Heathcote was also the village blacksmith, postman etc., and had only one or two teeth showing through a soot-blackened face, a cackling laugh, and a Derbyshire accent worth recording for posterity. He must have known my maternal grandmother quite well, as she grew up in a cottage almost opposite the forge, and her father had been the village tailor, parish clerk, commission agent, local newspaper correspondent et al. (A lot of multitasking went on in those days.) When the forge was still open, I used to go and watch Mr H. shoeing horses sometimes – the heat, the noise, the flying sparks and the smells of hot horses, hot metal and leather aprons were fascinating, if a little scary – but can't remember when it closed and/or Mr Heathcote retired. It must have been after then that Mr Summers started sweeping our chimney. The forge was next to the Joiners Arms pub and is now part of their car park.

Mr Heathcote lived in a cottage further up the hill on the opposite side. The cottage where my grandmother was born was a little lower down, almost opposite the strange little building which housed the chalybeate, or mineral-water well. This had dried up many years before, after an earth tremor. Near it was Quarndon Old Church, a ruin almost totally covered in ivy so that it looked like an old tree. Tess, and later Margaret and other friends and I, used to play in the churchyard sometimes, fascinated by the old gravestones and half-open tombs which were there. Disappointingly, they have now all been tidied away, though the church tower is even more invisible than ever. Is nothing sacred?!

At the back of the Old Church was the Old Church House, occupied by an elderly lady called, according to my grandmother, Daisy Voss. We used to go and peep in the ruinous outhouses which surrounded it, and Mrs Voss would occasionally chase us out with a broom. She was very agile and I think she actually enjoyed it as much as we did, since we never did any harm. My grandmother mentioned us to her once, and she just laughed. The Old Church House was a pretty building with chapel-style arched windows. Grandma's cottage was Vine Cottage, higher up the hill, almost opposite the Joiners Arms. From here, one day, when my grandmother was six days old, so the story went, her mother had abandoned her husband and two children and departed for a life of mystery and subterfuge. She never returned, although strange rumours persisted, but it was some hundred years later that her great-granddaughter – a nosy, interfering dirt-digger of a writer, namely me – discovered the real story, or at least about 95% of it. And, boy, what a story it is! Bigamous marriages, false names, alternative families, emigration, ignominious return…

History has a way of catching us out, and when I did finally obtain, online, an image of my naughty, long-lost great-grandmother, she was not quite the sultry, slightly resentful pre-Raphaelite beauty I'd imagined, but an older, mature woman posing by a vintage car, wearing an elegant stitched beret and a big fur coat, a self-satisfied cross between Queen Mary and Bonnie Parker.

FOUR

Christmases Past

My first remembered Christmas was my first remembered actual event; those pink lights shining on snow from the back of a taxi, crossing what were then known as the Arterial Roads – now better known as the Derby Ring Road – on the way to Grandma Neal's dark and scary house near the Cavendish on Stenson Road, Normanton. I realise now that it must have been the terrible winter of 1946–47, when the snow was as high as the tops of the hedges along Kedleston Road where my other grandmother lived. I would have been two years old. In Grandma Neal's middle room, which was the darkest part of the house apart from the hall and the attic, was my mother's original piano, and I remember my grandfather sitting me on his knee and playing 'It Came Upon a Midnight Clear'. Whether that was the same occasion, I am not sure, but I do remember the carol. He was the only person apart from Mum who played that piano. Mum had another piano; a baby grand which Dad's family had given her as a wedding present when they moved into their new house in Allestree. It took up most of our front room, and I used to drop my toy cars under the lid. This didn't make me particularly popular or do much for the tone of the piano. The only other thing I can remember about that first Christmas was wailing in the middle of Christmas dinner for some reason, and someone, probably Grandma, saying, rather fussily, "Oh, she doesn't like the goose!"

"Or maybe the apple sauce," somebody added. But I've no idea what it was. I was probably just being a pain.

The middle room in Grandma's house was seldom used, probably on account of its relative darkness, being an L-shaped terraced house, and the fire only seemed to be lit at Christmas. My mother used to worry that the piano would get damp and go out of tune and should be moved into the sunnier front room. The piano brooded in there like a very large black beetle. However, it sounded fine when my grandfather played it that day. Grandpa Neal died when I was eleven, which was very sad, as he was a lovely man. My other grandfather had died more than ten years before I was born, so he was the only grandfather I knew.

The kitchen, where we all ate at Stenson Road, was a large, pleasant room with a massive blackleaded Aga-type range, but a gas cooker had been installed in the adjoining scullery which was now used for most of the cooking, although I think the range may have been hauled into used for special occasions like Christmas. It would probably have suited my grandmother better, as she was a dab hand at explosions and other domestic mishaps, and blew herself across the kitchen with the aid of the gas stove on a number of occasions, on one of them via a celluloid-handled knife she'd left in a pan of hot fat. How she lived to be ninety unscathed I'll never know. Later, when we'd moved to the bungalow, just after the Little Brown Man incident, she blew up our living room by chucking a hearing-aid battery onto the fire, wrapped in a screw of paper. It scorched the ceiling and set fire to the hearth rug and really made our Christmas Day.

Most Christmases, however, at least when I was small, tended to be spent at my father's mother's house on Kedleston Road, though it was actually much smaller and the family larger. My Neal grandparents had begun to spend their Christmases at a hotel, which they continued to do until my grandfather died. My mother only had two brothers who, when I was small, were still single, but my father's three brothers were married, or one separated, with older children, and there were quite a lot of us in the small semi on Kedleston Road. This grandmother had risen in status from Brook Street where she'd worked in a cotton mill in Derby's West End, to a terraced house in Chester Green after her marriage, later to a large house on Duffield Road with uniformed servants, then, after her husband's death at barely fifty, to a smaller house near Broadway before the pre-War semi which became her final home. "Clogs to carriages and back to clogs again in three generations," as my dad once said, and it was true. Although, only two in our case, sadly. We did have some fun, though, until Gran really got too old and frail to have us all there, and Christmases tended to migrate to our house (by this time a two-bedroomed bungalow), at least for the grandmothers and ourselves. Uncle Ben, my dad's older brother, sometimes joined us, as well as our elderly Scottish neighbour. On one occasion, my mother left a large bowl of turkey fat outside on the back step to cool – what *do* you do with turkey fat? – and when she came back later, the dog had walloped the lot. And did she turn a hair? Not one. We hardly dared let her back in the house for fear of dire results, but that dog had a stomach of iron.

This would have been in the days after food rationing had ended, or we probably wouldn't have managed a turkey. Although my grandfather had been a wholesale grocer and certain things were not so hard to obtain, I'm not sure what happened re. meat and poultry. One thing that did happen during food rationing, though, was that one day Dad came home, delighted, with a large box of chocolate biscuits a colleague on the railway had given him; an unwanted gift from a relative in the US, or maybe it was South Africa, who worked in a biscuit factory or something. Naturally, we were also delighted, not having seen many chocolate biscuits for a very long time; in my case, probably never. Many years later, the same colleague was done for theft of goods from the railway and locked up for some time. He'd been doing it for years, apparently. Dad, who was one of those people who tend not to think ill of anyone without good reason, was mortified. I think he probably spent some time afterwards worrying in case a heavy hand fell upon his shoulder and a voice said, "Excuse me, sir, but did you once accept a large box of knocked-off biscuits around the year 1950?" But I'm glad to say, it never did!

Of course, one of the important things that happened at Christmas, once you were of school age, was the much-dreaded, yet eagerly anticipated, school play. This was usually, though not always, a Nativity play. I always secretly wanted to play the Virgin Mary, but I never did. Clearly I was not Virgin Mary material.

Somehow, there is always something very touching about seeing tiny children re-enacting this timeless, strangely humble, yet mysterious Middle Eastern story. Vaguely, I seem to remember being a shepherd in a dressing gown, with the obligatory tea towel on my head. Once we did Hiawatha (more dressing gowns to the fore) and my mother made me a papoose carrier to put on my back with a baby doll in it, which obviously nobody else had, and I was very pleased with it until Sir Smyth, our manic but very small teacher from Northern Ireland, a sort of Reverend Ian Paisley in miniature, broke the doll's legs by grabbing it to push me along to where he wanted me to stand. Needless to say, we never got an apology out of him, not that anyone could ever understand anything he said anyway. He put me off arithmetic and Belfast accents for life. Perhaps it was only the top class, though, who did a really serious Nativity play, when everyone commented on how wonderfully mature the girl who played the Blessed Virgin Mary seemed, and how pure she looked, crossing her hands so demurely across her as yet non-existent bosom, as she declaimed, "*And from henceforth, all generations shall call me blessed...*" That girl later came to live near us, and when we started at grammar school the following year, we became friends for a while, doing our homework together while listening to Radio Luxembourg, until one day she made an obscene phone call to our newly installed telephone... And that was the end of that beautiful friendship, really. One boy, a bit of a local delinquent type, made a truly terrifying King Herod, with a mad fright wig that look suspiciously like a mop head. Excellent typecasting, we all thought. In later years he amazed everyone by gaining an Oxbridge scholarship. The Blessed Virgin Mary, on the other hand, who'd been put into a super-fast stream because she seemed so bright, accelerated rapidly downhill and was last seen behind the counter of a record shop being languid and eccentric and pretending she didn't know me. Or ever made peculiar phone calls.

Obviously, in those days, nobody ever explained anything to children, and I puzzled for ages about where Orientar was (i.e. where We Three Kings came from). But, like all

Derbyshire children, I knew that the Baby Jesus was wrapped in Swadlincote and laid in a manger. The only thing that confused me was whether a Swadlincote was actually a garment, named after the place (after all, there used to be a Chesterfield overcoat), or whether Swadlincote, known only to me as a place not far away where my dad went to work on odd occasions, and usually known simply as 'Swad', was a place where they wrapped babies. To this day, I still visualise a sign that says *SWADLINCOTE* with a small, neatly wrapped baby under it…

Another well-remembered Christmas Past came many years later, when I was working at the library in Bold Lane in Derby, and is worth remembering for its exquisite awfulness. I'd like to say it was Dickensian, though the building actually dated from 1760. Still, the principle's the same. It had what my dad would have described as that 'Christmas Day in the Workhouse' flavour. There were about five of us at the time, all more or less anarchists of one kind or another. Courtesy of Derbyshire County Council, with Dickensian frugality, we shivered in the cold as we tried to warm a few mince pies on the radiators (a fruitless task, in fact) and availed ourselves of a small bottle of pretty dreadful wine I'd managed to obtain from the nearest off-licence. Not liking sherry, I think I'd gone for something labelled muscatel, but it had more of the gloopiness of syrup of figs laced with something like moth repellent. No readers had been seen for some time – it was Christmas Eve, as I recall – and as we crumbled a mince pie or two onto the lino and hesitated over the muscatel, the shuffle of the regional librarian's tiny feet went unheard outside our door. A small, huffy woman, all bust and indignation, it was highly unlikely she'd come to wish us the season's greetings, so more probably she had something to complain about.

Clearly the Bacchanalian debauchery of mince pies on the pipes and muscatel was too much for her and she exploded with wrath like an overwrought pressure cooker. We watched in amazement as she ranted and raved until steam came out of her ears, accusing us of being a disgrace to our profession, then stomped off like Rumpelstiltskin, back down the stairs. There was a hushed pause for several minutes before one of our number murmured, "And a very merry Christmas to you too, Mrs D!", before we fell about among the mince-pie crumbs. Apart from unwisely attending something called a Social Evening at Matlock, during which nobody spoke, that was about the height of organised leisure activity I remember during my years in the library service.

Other Bank Holidays never seemed to feature in my memory as much as Christmas. Easter was always freezing cold and horrible, Whit was something slightly nebulous and unmemorable, and the August Bank Holiday so wet it became a national joke to such an extent that the government eventually changed it from the beginning to the end of August. Locally, the other weather black spot was Carriage and Wagon fortnight, which I think may have coincided with the original August Bank Holiday and was reputed to be so awful that nobody else in Derby *ever* took their holidays then. Since Dad was a relief clerk on the railway, this meant he had to do other people's jobs while they were away, so he was usually working then anyway. This became a bone of contention with the school authorities, who were just as officious then as they are today, to be honest, and always kicked up because we needed to take our annual break when other people didn't. Persuading our vindictive headmistress that this was not some frivolous choice but a contractual necessity always proved difficult, especially as she didn't seem to like me much. She'd long since taken an exception to me, since I had quite a bit of time off due to illness, and once sent the schools inspector round to the house when I was in hospital, a fact she knew full well, as a demoralisation gesture. Whenever I was off sick, she referred to it as "another little holiday", sympathy not being her strong point. You had to be either very rich or very underprivileged to be in favour with Miss J, in which case you'd be either fawned upon as a possible cash cow or hideously patronised. Since I was neither of these things, I was beneath her contempt. Holidays were always a bone of contention, therefore, and something I didn't like to mention, with or without the customary letter from my parents. Bank Holidays, however, were different. Apparently. To me the words 'Bank Holiday' meant a day when people were allowed to go out into the countryside and sit on banks. It made perfect sense to me.

FIVE

Strange Neighbours...

One day when I was about eight, I was playing with a girl who lived in the next street. I didn't know her very well, as she went to a different school, but our parents knew each other and we always said hello in passing. The only other thing I remember about her was a rather portly sausage dog which may or may not have been present on the occasion when I saw The Mysterious Ape-Man.

I was in the back garden of this house in Hollies Road when my friend decided to go into the house to get a drink of water. I waited outside, and as I looked back towards the house, something in the upstairs window of the house next door caught my eye. A weird figure of a man-like creature was standing there, looking at me. It was naked, as far as I could see; pinkish-skinned but covered with fine white hair, and had no neck at all. Its face simply flowed into its shoulders, which were massive, like those of some kind of ape. I can't remember its actual features, other than that they were vaguely apelike, and it had tiny but very bright eyes, which positively glittered as it stared right at me in what seemed to be a very hostile manner. The eyes seemed to catch the light in a bizarre kind of way, and the whole effect was very frightening indeed. It stood and stared at me for what seemed like a very long moment, before moving away from the window just as my friend reappeared in the garden. I was too traumatised to say anything or even mention it to her, and I never did find out who or what it was, but it certainly made a lasting impression. To this day, I am still curious. I am certain it was not just a normal overweight human being, although, at the tender age of eight, my experience of seeing gents with no clothes on was somewhat limited, but whatever it was, it didn't seem quite human. The family who lived there had a son with a slight physical disability, but his appearance was not in any way unusual. Was there another family member with some kind of disfigurement? I never dared to try and find out. Strangely enough, only a few years ago, I saw a man in the town with a similar disability, in that his head seemed to flow into his chest. He was chatting to someone in the street, though had a pleasant, friendly face, whereas the figure in the window looked very aggressive indeed. I suppose I'll never know.

On thinking over the strangeness of neighbours, it was mainly the womenfolk who tended towards weirdness. The men, as I think I've said before, were a greyish, crepuscular lot, rarely seen during daylight hours – well, not by small children, anyway. On looking back, there were a lot of single women around then; war widows in particular, or women who'd lost their fiancés during the conflict, or unmarried mothers (who were never treated well), and some cases were quite sad. Some were nice. Some were bitter. Some were definitely scary. Many of them had an active dislike of children. Come to think of it, some of the married ones *with* children were often the worst in the Department of Sadism and Vicious Behaviour, so let's not be picky...

I remember a woman leaning over her gate in Allestree Lane and screaming abuse at me, when I was seven or eight, accusing me of 'stealing her daughter's friends'. I was somewhat confused, since I didn't have much to do with her daughter or the friend I was supposed to have stolen. The daughter was a kid I'd tried to make friends with in the past and once invited to tea, whereupon she'd moaned and whined and complained about the food, causing my mother to comment afterwards, "What an awful girl! Don't ask her again!" I didn't. I gave mother and daughter a very wide berth after the verbal abuse incident, though I'm sorry to say another friend and I were not averse to making the occasional snide remark in her direction. Unfortunately, I was to bump into her again, much later in life, and learned that several members of the family did, in fact, have mental health issues, but that's not easy to understand when you're seven. At the time, I was quite frightened.

Allestree boasted a number of Miss Havisham figures, most notably the mysterious black-clad woman in the semi-ruinous house near the Post Office in Allestree Lane, who has inspired a short story or two; the White-Faced Lady of Duffield Road (ditto), who powdered her face with flour or possibly some form of stucco, and always wore riding breeches; several Blanche DuBois types; and a number of Mrs Danvers. The Lady of Allestree Lane was also reputed to have been a housekeeper who had been left the house, but not the money for its upkeep. She was not really scary, however; merely mysterious. Wicked Stepmothers abounded, while several children at our school had mothers akin to Mrs Williams, the monumental mother in Dylan Thomas's story who didn't like *The Peaches*. All in all, it's no wonder I became a writer.

Considering the times we grew up in, it's surprising there weren't a lot more damaged people around. Strangely enough, despite the fact that there must have been many people who had been mentally affected by the War, I felt much safer then than I do now. I suppose we were shielded from it all, to a certain extent, whereas those who'd grown up in a time of conflict simply thought – according to one cousin, anyway – that life had always been like that. Nonetheless, two of my parents' friends committed suicide because of dreadful wartime experiences, and a devoutly Christian friend of my mother's, who survived the torpedoing of a hospital ship, was so traumatised she never entered a church again. But these were not people I knew and were seldom spoken about, and their stories were not told until much later.

Several children I knew seemed to have no fathers, and I remember one boy saying his father had died in the War before he was born. I simply couldn't grasp this concept at all, at the age of five or six. His mother had since remarried, and I remember always being slightly puzzled that he and his mother had different surnames. Many women, obviously, had lost either a husband or a fiancé in the War, and I remember one lady in particular whose parents ran the baker's shop where we bought our bread. Her name was Nancy, and she had known my mother since childhood. She was a good-looking woman with golden-brown eyes, like pansies, and always had a slightly sad look. There must have been many like her. I was surprised to learn she only died recently at a great age.

Around this time there were many adopted children about as well, but no one ever talked about their background and it seemed to be the rule that knowledge of birth parents etc. should be kept secret. This was deemed to be better for the child. Why this should have been the case, I can't imagine, unless there was something extremely traumatic to hide, and it took over sixty years to discover what happened to a cousin of my mother's who'd been orphaned by the previous war. Even her own sister went to her grave haunted by never knowing what had happened to her. This was before the days of an official adoption policy, when information was even more scanty, and if I and her grandson hadn't both chanced to start searching on an ancestry research website around the same time, we might never have known.

SIX

Holidays

I can remember little about my earliest holidays except a boarding house in Bridlington, with no carpets on the stairs and the sound of soldiers' boots rattling up and down them. Once we met a family from Southport, on the opposite side of the country, with whom we became friends and whom we later visited at their home in Ainsdale, which I can just remember, a few years later. Sandhills, snail shells and light aircraft are about all I remember, plus everyone running outside to view a jet plane, quite a novelty then, and seeing an oil tanker out of Liverpool Docks, the biggest thing I'd ever seen. Then from there, a visit to the Lake District, where it rained so much we couldn't get out of the train. Seeing automatic train doors for the first time, opening to more rain at Preston – the only interesting thing I saw all day. Another time, another visit, this time to either Scarborough or Bridlington, with a family from Allestree who lived quite close. I still see the daughter occasionally, who was about a year older than me, and we laugh about it, but actually can't remember any details. Holidays were very basic then. There is one photo taken at some unidentified holiday spot, showing my mother, looking rather glamorous in summer dress with a hat pushed back against her shoulders, sitting on a clifftop, and me peering through the long grass at her feet, aged about two, scowling like some small, malevolent Highland cow.

Something I do remember vividly was being on Derby Midland Station, still with its damaged glass roof (a victim of air raids in both World Wars), and being startled by a violently loud engine noise – not the steam locomotives that we were used to, far from quiet in themselves, but something that caused the whole structure, rickety as it was, to vibrate. "That," shouted my dad, seeing our alarm, "is *Diesel No. 10,000*!" Since I've read only recently that LMS *Diesel 10,000* first left Derby Loco Works in December 1947, I conclude that either we were there at that time, or more probably en route to somewhere in the spring of 1948, in which case I would have been four. Either way, at the time I thought it was the loudest thing I'd ever heard. To be honest, none of my memories of the original Derby Station are particularly endearing. I described it once as having all the charm of a derelict abattoir, and I don't think I was exaggerating. Looking at really old photographs, I can see that it did once have an imposing air about it, especially the frontage, but bombs, accidental fires and years of general neglect had wreaked havoc with all that and I honestly only remember it as a dark, dismal dump, damp, draughty and dilapidated. One day when my father arrived at work in one of the main buildings, a large coping stone had fallen from the roof straight through his desk. While there was much wailing and gnashing of teeth from local historians and others when it was finally demolished, I can't say I really missed it. My only consolation about our totally depressing station was that Nottingham's was infinitely worse.

Another memory regarding stations, Nottingham in particular, was of seeing the Queen and Princess Margaret at Nottingham Victoria Station en route to the Royal Show, which was being held at Wollaton Park. According to the records, this was in July 1955, in which case, unless it was a Saturday, Dad must have wangled me a day off school. The record claims they were received at Nottingham Midland Station, but I remember it definitely as Nottingham Victoria, which was Nottingham's posh station, huge and cavernous but certainly impressive. That bit the dust even before most of Derby Midland Station, which presumably had been *our* posh station pre-Luftwaffe days. Nottingham Victoria linked up with Derby Friargate, which was our lesser station on the LNER, small, verging on the rural, and smelling faintly of fish. Friargate was the station people used to embark from when heading for the holiday resorts of the East Coast, as I'm sure we would have done. Derby Friargate, entered by a gloomy, gaslit tunnel, closed in 1963, but bits of it still remain, mouldering amidst untended former goods yards and its one redeeming architectural feature: Friargate Bridge. Nottingham Victoria vanished forever beneath the Victoria Shopping Centre.

Today both Midland Stations still exist, Derby's now behind a modern facade; the platforms, still strictly sans the original Platform 5 (bombed in January 1941), as ever lacking in charm, but at least relatively clean and light, and revamped again since I commenced writing. Nottingham Midland, always a disgrace for a city of its size, was recently renovated at enormous cost, although if you were unwise enough to want to go to Norwich, as I did (I don't recommend it unless you have time on your hands), you still had to wait on a pile of loose chippings. Ironically, almost as soon as the renovation was finished, some maniac set fire to it.

The first real holiday I remember, when we stayed in an actual hotel – had we come into money or what? – was at Mortehoe in North Devon, right opposite Lundy Island. It would have been 1951 or 1952. I remember seeing fuchsias for the first time, and red valerian, and thinking, or someone saying, *They grow in Spain.* Why did this impress me so much? Devon was warm and wonderful, and I loved it. The only other thing I can remember about the hotel was that they had a dinner gong; very impressive to me at that time. It made the whole building shake. And my dad singing silly songs to me as we came up from the beach for the evening meal. When I went back there, years later, as a teenager, the hotel was still there, too expensive for our humble means by then, and the cliff path which led from their gardens had collapsed onto the beach. It was there, as a teenager, close to Morte Point, that I saw that rare natural occurrence, a green flash, when suddenly, just as the sun goes down, the whole world seems to turn an amazing translucent turquoise green. Having just read up on the green flash phenomenon, I'm surprised to learn that it usually appears as a sort of bright green blur above the sun as it hits the horizon, rather than illuminating everything around as we saw it that evening, when the whole headland, the vegetation and our own faces were bathed in a pale, clear bluish green, rather like that colour photographers call cyan. We assumed it was caused by the sun shining through the water, but apparently the actual green flash is caused by refraction. So we must have seen something quite special. One local person told us it's something you only see once in a lifetime.

Then coronation year, 1953, and my dad's holiday time meant, much to my school's annoyance and my delight, that we would be away for the school coronation ceremony, during which I would have had to march round the playground holding hands with a small boy I hated. Thanks, Dad! We were back for the actual coronation, though, but more of that later. So, on a damp and misty morning, we found ourselves on Penzance Station accompanied by the smell of fish and gas, wondering if we had made a horrible mistake. We hadn't.

After half an hour or so, a green-and-cream bus rumbled up, operated somewhat erratically by a very chatty Johnny and Charlie, and deposited us at some crossroads by a chapel at Drift, halfway to Land's End. The sun came out and we found ourselves outside a white cottage, occupied by a cheerful, energetic Cornishwoman, her small, very freckled son, and her useless (I quote) husband who spent most of his time, apparently, on a quay somewhere propping up a bollard, while the missus ran the B&B and a market garden where she grew veg and daffodils.

There we returned for many a year, sometimes with our Allestree friends and their small daughters of dog-biscuit fame, who would drive down from Derby. They would bring our dog down with them, and by this time the children had luckily gone off dog biscuits so there was no fighting over provisions. Drift was actually several miles from the sea, so we all piled into the car most days and headed for whichever beach took our fancy. On looking at old photos, the first car seems to have been a Rover, built like a tank but getting on a bit; and the one I remember most – and who wouldn't? – was the dreaded Standard Vanguard, possibly the most uncomfortable car designed by man. The Standard Vanguard looked like a pregnant Volkswagen and didn't have much going for it except that it was big. Big enough to accommodate four adults, three children and a dog, in considerable discomfort, it had a ridge across the middle of the back seat which people drew straws not to have to sit on. However, it did get us all from A to B (and knowing Cornish roads, that was usually round via Z), and you could get one hell of a lot in the boot, so I suppose it did have its practicalities. Passers-by stood agog in amazement at the amount of stuff we kept on removing from the bowels of that car. It was just a bummer to sit in, in every sense of the word.

One of my fond memories of going down to the West Country is of taking the overnight train down from Derby to Penzance. I'm not sure where this started off from, but presumably much further north, and it was often fairly full when we got on. There were no sleepers in those days – you just stayed in your seat, which as far as I recall wasn't bookable in advance, either. Usually there was room enough for one couple and a child, if only just, but on one occasion, we'd just got ourselves settled when a huge older lady, whom I remember distinctly as wearing blood-coloured pendant earrings and a dustbin-lid hat, accompanied by another woman we presumed was her spinster daughter, both equally grim, barged into our compartment and plonked herself into the tiny space next to my poor mother with an audible splat, her elbows pinioning Mum and the person on her other side firmly in their seats. "This'll be nice all the way to Penzance!" she announced, as her daughter did the same thing on the opposite side.

As the train started to move, Dad sprang into action. "I'll find you a seat!" he announced, and grabbed their luggage and vanished down the corridor with it. The two women extricated themselves like someone taking two spoonfuls out of a very firm jelly and hurtled after him and out of sight, leaving the other passengers falling about laughing. Dad returned after about five minutes, slightly flushed but smiling benignly; another good job done.

Once we'd got through the smoke-blackened canyons of Birmingham New Street, waited for the engaging sound of the *Lickey Banker* helping us up the incline, and were back on the level again, we were soon heading towards ghostly night-time Cheltenham and Gloucester, then Bristol with beautiful Temple Meads Station, where we sometimes had to change, still proud amongst the bomb damage; Exeter, then Plymouth and over the mighty Tamar Bridge, looking at the distant shipping far below. Then we were truly in Cornwall, which emerged through early-morning mist to the sound of milk churns clonging on platforms.

Even then, in the mid 1950s, Cornwall was largely undiscovered, and our time was often spent on almost empty beaches, and many towns and villages were very untouristy and, in some cases, quite run-down. I sometimes wish it was still that way. It really was another country. Once, my parents and I decided to visit the ancient British village of Chysauster, somewhere on the moors behind Penzance. I can't remember how we got there, but after looking round the village site, which had only recently been excavated, we walked off down a long and empty road which seemed to be miles from anywhere. It was red hot and the country was in the middle of a drought. There seemed to be no signposts and, as far as I recall, we had no food, drink or map with us. We just kept on walking. No sign of habitation anywhere. Eventually one of us spotted some telephone wires, humming as they always did in the hot south-west wind, and we noticed they led along a track to a building. We walked along until we reached it, only to find an abandoned wartime installation of some kind and a dead end. Disconsolate, we walked back to the road and kept on going in what we hoped was the right direction, hopefully back towards Penzance. Still no sign of habitation. After another mile or so, we came upon a dilapidated house with a triangle of grass in front, where we asked for directions and a drink of water. A woman and a child were there, dressed in very ragged clothes, and I remember particularly that the small girl was wearing old-fashioned black shoes with square buckles, very dusty. "We've got no water," she said. "I can give you a glass of milk, if you like." She didn't look as though she could spare it, and none of us really drank milk anyway, so, feeling a bit guilty, we thanked her and headed in the vague direction she'd pointed. They seemed like people from some long-ago famine.

After another mile or so, we came to a small village. At first, it seemed hopeful – cottages, a faded green where three lanes met, a shop. Utterly silent. We went up to the shop, peered through the dirty glass, saw nothing but an empty counter, mouse-chewed paper, bits of rubble. The houses were the same. Gaping windows, missing slates. The village was deserted. To this day, I'll never know its name or where it was. Years later, returning with my husband and children, we drove around from Gulval where we were staying in search of it, without success, though we found the house with the triangle of grass, a ruin now, with rafters sticking through the roof. But on that hot, dry day, all those years ago, we kept on walking.

Eventually, we came to a larger village with a crossroads and a church, which I have yet to identify, though online checking has just led me to Ludgvan on the B3309 – which looks like the most likely candidate – and I vaguely remember buying a packet of biscuits or something and some lemonade and sitting on a wall occupied by tiny red spiders, before heading on our way again. My mother seems to have taken a photo of me and Dad, which I still have, standing wearily by the signpost there. It was the only signpost we'd seen all day and the inscription is barely legible. Presumably we took the road pointing towards Gulval and Penzance. No buses, no mobile phones then. However, there *was* a phone box – I have the photo – but who would we ring? No one even had a house phone then! Before long it started to get dark, and by now were beginning to get worried, when car headlights appeared. It was our friend who'd come out looking for us in the Vanguard. And were we grateful!

A bypass cuts across the area now, and I imagine most of the signposts, largely removed during the Second World War, have long since been put back. At least, I hope so! Drift now has a reservoir, though it's some distance from the village as we knew it. Thirty or so years ago, passing the Drift crossroads with my husband and children, I simply had to stop and cautiously call at the cottage. Our old landlady's son was still living there, and his wife, who answered the door, told us she'd remarried and gone to live in Glasgow. Useless Eustace, presumably, had gone on to his reward by this time. I didn't dare to ask. It still looked the same. The field with its gentle, soft-eyed Channel Island cattle was still there, and the lane, with its high banks packed with ivy, pennywort and honeysuckle, looked as remote and untouched as ever.

The other thing I forgot to mention was the *Warspite*. On that first visit, through the mist and drizzle shrouding Mount's Bay, slewed across it like some giant dinosaur were the rusting remains of a battleship. It was the *Warspite*, a veteran of the First World War and later the Second, which had broken free on its way to the breaker's yard as a final act of defiance and resisted all attempts to move it. Year after year, it got smaller, as the tugs and breakers swarmed around it, picking at its bones, until finally, one year, it had gone. But I remembered it, mainly, I suppose, because, even in decay, it had seemed somehow quite beautiful. Many years later, waiting for a P&O ferry in Portsmouth, I noticed a model of a battleship in the museum there. From the far side of the room, I said, "That's the *Warspite*!" It was, too.

Cornwall seemed magical then, with its jewel-like colours, when the sea was always turquoise or lapis or jade green, and the high-banked lanes were studded with flowers and big stripy snail shells. Cornwall smelled wonderful, too, with the salt tang of the sea, the scent of turf and flowers, and the smell of warm granite. But then it was wilderness, a desert of moorland and standing stones, abandoned mineshafts and engine houses, tumbled cottages, tiny coves and empty beaches, with a silence and a magic never to be regained.

SEVEN

Shops and Shopkeepers, Strange and Sinister

When I first moved to Mickleover, where I live now, I remember going into the nearest shop and unwisely asking for a packet of Bisto or something equally innocuous. It was about 1969 and before political correctness or customer services had been invented.

"No," came the heart-warming reply. Not *Sorry, we're just out of that*, or *Can I offer you something else, perhaps?* Just "No."

And whoever it was carried on filling in their pools coupon or combing out their nits or whatever they'd been doing before I was so insolent as to open their door.

Ah, roll on Tesco, I'd have said, had I known what was coming. Presumably they didn't know what was coming either, since, if they'd made the teeniest effort, perhaps their shop would still be operational instead of gutted and combined with the bank next door. When I called at the local Post Office to send a letter to somewhere in Europe, I was screamed at by a harridan out of a *Monty Python* sketch because I'd put it in an airmail envelope. Since then, the bank has also, alas, closed, and the Post Office has moved over the road, where it is now run by normal people.

When I was growing up, across the other side of town in the 1950s, Allestree was still a developing suburb, a mile from the old village. Neither fish nor fowl to the old villagers, we did at least have our own shops along Allestree Lane, most of which had been built just before the Second World War. They may have been quite new then, but they, too, had that Royston Vasey flavour. The grocery store was run by a thin, middle-aged couple so chillingly superior their premises needed no refrigeration. I only ever entered their shop in the event of a serious emergency. Luckily, since my grandfather was a wholesale grocer, most of our provisions could be supplied by him, but there were occasions when a visit to Mr and Mrs P became a hideous inevitability. This was generally to buy eggs, which rarely made it all the way home, since Mr and Mrs P, with their usual curl of the lip, only ever put them in a paper bag. Whether this was because egg boxes hadn't yet been invented or because the Ps were too frugal to spare one, I'm not sure. On reflection, I'm surprised they didn't just hand them over to me one at a time. They had a pale-faced, sarcastic son of about my age who was rude to me at school, and an older daughter, the only one of the family who could manage a smile.

On the opposite corner was a butcher's shop, run by a chunky, Brylcreemed gent called Gordon. Gordon knew about as much about meat as I know about thermodynamics, and his idea of a chop was something you hit with a cleaver until it fell to bits. The floor was coated thickly with the sawdust reputed to go into his sausages. Gordon also specialised in short change, though whether this was accidental was open to debate. On the whole, though, he was a kindly soul, if just a wee bit on the dodgy side, and it was impossible not to like him. Everyone said hello to Gordon, though avoided him like the plague if they wanted actual meat, since his produce was awful.

Further on was a newsagent's run by a couple called Clarke. Mrs Clarke lived in a turmoil of perpetual excitement and spoke very quickly in a high-pitched, enthusiastic voice, and was nothing if not polite. In fact, she addressed even the smallest of children as sir or madam, and happily handed over the smallest halfpenny chew with the maximum of ceremony. She wore a painted-on triangular smile on her tiny triangular face beneath a frizz of peroxided hair, and her anxiety to please was exhausting. She was, in fact, a sort of East Midlands Gracie Allen, and I don't think she ever stopped talking from dawn till dusk. Mr Clarke, on the other hand, was rarely heard to utter a word, not even "Say goodnight to the folks, Gracie", and, combined with the exertion of being married to Mrs Clarke, plus the early hours newsagents have to keep, probably suffered from permanent fatigue. Prior to this, the shop was owned by a grumpy couple, inclined to tick off children who hung about reading the comics displayed on a rack outside. (We must have had drier weather then.) Here we could catch up on the exploits of Dan Dare and the dreaded Mekon, which, being girls, we weren't supposed to read. Gosh, it was sexist in those days. ('We', by this stage, refers to me and the previously mentioned Margaret, who lived further down the Lane.) Since we were usually asked to desist before we'd got to the inside page, we never did get to finish one. Vaguely, I remember a wizened granny, too, who, after they had moved to the next village, excelled herself by chucking a cup of scalding tea in the face of a would-be till robber. "And good for her," we all cried.

Further along the road, a hardware shop opened, run by a hawk-faced, gloomy couple, relatively normal except that she wore dangly purple earrings. From there, I would carry refilled cans of smelly paraffin which clonked against my knees all the way home. Then, between them and the Clarkes, a new shop opened, run by an affable young man named Barry. He was a grocer of a sort – a 'packet grocer', my grandfather would have called him – and knew about as much about the grocery trade as Gordon knew about meat, but what he lacked in knowledge, he made up for in charm, and even the proverbial short change was replenished with a friendly smile. (Barry couldn't add up, either.) Customers flocked to Barry like refugees from a police state. Above the shop was a hairdressing salon, run by a Miss Williams, and later, I think, by Barry's wife.

Between the Lane and the old village was a tiny, bow-fronted corner shop that stood on its own. The shopkeeper was a massive lady called Mrs Brock (actually Brocklehurst, in full), who loomed over the counter like Les Dawson in drag. Sweets came off the ration when I was nine, which is why my generation have such lousy teeth, and the single attraction of Mrs Brock's was that it was the only place where you could get an ice cream on a Sunday. If it hadn't been for that, I doubt anyone would ever have gone there, since she scared the life out of all of us. Mrs Brock's stinginess was legendary, and she used to charge threepence for the ice cream, a penny each for the wafers and another penny for putting them on for you. She had a bosom like a barrage balloon and her husband was a clown. (I have this on good authority, by the way, improbable though it sounds.) No one ever saw him, however, as he was permanently on duty elsewhere, probably attempting to undo the emotional damage done to small children by his wife.

Further on into the village itself, a few shops lay either side of the A6, but the far side was alien territory to us. There was a butcher's, another grocer's, a wool shop, a non-dispensing chemist (where the local lads allegedly went for their 'weekend supplies', although of course we were too young and innocent to know about such things), and a Co-op, though we never went there. There was even a chip shop, but thanks to public morality, or possibly just rationing, it was only allowed to open one night a week. On our side, however, there was a garage, a Post Office and a shoe repairer. This was Mr Jennings, the cobbler, a taciturn gent with curly hair and glasses, who was so used to kids from our school going in there to have our bulging schoolbags sewn up that he just took the satchel off us with a disparaging grunt and handed us a ticket. His shop was really just a hut, its walls studded with heels, soles and blakeys, also known as segs, and smelled of wood, glue and hot rubber.

Allestree never had a bakery. Decent bread could only be obtained from a small shop in town, presided over by a scowling woman with a moustache and a hairnet, or another near Five Lamps owned by the family of Mum's old school friend Nancy. Their bread was wonderful. Below the Markeaton Hotel, on the Kedleston Road, past the vinegar factory and opposite the market garden where my mother used to work, was Buxton's, a grocer's shop which also had a bakery. Their bread was good, too, though rather soft in texture, and had a distinctive teacakey flavour and a slightly winey smell which was quite unique. Everyone remembered the smell of Buxton's bread. After my grandfather died, it was Buxton's who delivered our groceries every week. Between our village and Darley Abbey, on the A6, was the Court Cafe, a pretty building with a separate kiosk for sweets and pop, which had a wooden verandah. This seemed to be almost always closed, but, like Mrs Brock's, did have the advantage of occasionally being open on a Sunday. It smelled of wood and stale biscuits. Years later, it became a posh restaurant, but when I last went that way it was just a pile of rubble near the bypass, waiting to be cleared away.

The friendly local shop in Mickleover, when I eventually found it, whose rallying cry of "It's a bit over, alright?" was also well known, is now just somebody's house, closed after its owners retired and never reopened. They were kindly folk, despite the oft-quoted 'Arkwright' jokes, which amused them. The same fate has long befallen Barry's and all the local shops around Allestree except the hairdresser's, though not necessarily due to retirement. The original Allestree Lane Post Office, run by two older ladies, opposite the overgrown house where one of the Miss Havisham clones lived, was closed, and a new one opened at Park Farm Shopping Centre, which had obliterated Jonty Farmers. In a way, I'm sorry to see them go, but on the other hand, apart from Barry and Mrs Clarke, the owners didn't do much to endear themselves to their customers. If I was to write my own personal *Little Shop of Horrors*, I know where I'd set it…

Opposite the market garden where my mother worked as a land girl during the war years was a greengrocer's, owned by the same people, the Ride family. Occasionally, we would visit, as Buxton's, the bakery and grocery, was next door, and Mum would chat to Fred Ride, who'd run the nursery where she'd hoed the beans, picked the sprouts and spread the muck as a Land Girl all those years before. Fred was quite a character and had apparently somewhat resented my mother to begin with, doubtless passing her off as some poncey piano teacher who'd been fobbed off on him in the guise of an agricultural worker. He smoked an old clay pipe and would stand instructing her on what to do and deliberately blow pipe smoke in her face while doing so, until my otherwise quiet and ladylike mother had enough and took a mighty swipe at him. What he didn't know was that piano players tend to have hands like iron, and her dainty fist knocked the pipe clean out of his mouth and smashed it to bits. Both parties were equally surprised, I gather, and after that they became the best of friends. No pipe smoke passed into my mother's face again and a state of mutual respect was established.

Mum once told me that Fred had been through a dreadful experience as a boy sailor in the First World War when two ships collided in a Canadian harbour and exploded, killing almost everyone. Fred's hair had turned white with the shock and had stayed so for the rest of his life. Years later, I identified this as the terrible Halifax Explosion of 1917, when an ammunition ship, the *Mont-Blanc*, blew up and killed around two thousand people. No doubt that was one of the reasons why Fred was apt to be so moody. It's not the sort of trauma you can exactly put to the back of your mind.

Food was still rationed when I was very young and ration books had to be produced for every purchase. The books had to be replaced when the coupons were used up, and to do this we had to go into town to the General Post Office in Derby. The GPO was a large, cavernous building on the corner of St James Street and Victoria Street and was usually full of soldiers clomping about in heavy boots, which inevitably set our otherwise angelic dog off barking. Eventually my mother left him (and me) at my grandmother's on Kedleston Road until she came home. I used to sit by the little upstairs window, waiting for her to get off the trolley bus so we could walk the mile back up Allestree Lane home together. One day she came home and told me and Gran that the bells in town were all ringing because Princess Elizabeth had just had a baby boy. That would have been Prince Charles, and the year, 1948.

Many commodities were delivered then, and milk, in those days when I was very young, was often delivered by horse and cart, or in our case, by a farmer with a sort of pickup truck with a few churns on the back. The milk was ladled out into a jug with a dipper. Bottles came much later and my mother was always a little suspicious of them, as you never knew on whose unhygienic doorstep they'd been standing. Our milkman was called Mr Barker, who lived at Mugginton, a village some miles away in the direction of Ashbourne. In summer, he also sold damsons, and sometimes my grandfather would drive us out there to collect some to make into jam. After he gave up the milk round, a Mr Day took over, a wild and shaggy-looking man with snaggled teeth who my mother always thought looked like a cowboy; not the clean-cut Hollywood variety but the sort you sometimes saw in old photographs, dusty, crusty and smelling strongly of cow. He was actually quite a gentle soul, I believe, but after the mild-mannered Mr Barker, he did look a bit fearsome. He, too, drove a pickup truck, so we weren't privileged sufficiently to have a horse and cart, but the Co-op Dairy did, and the milk horse which visited houses further down the road was an endearing character called Pybus. Pybus was actually a skewbald, as I recall, rather than a piebald, having some brown patches, so his name may have been taken from a local family. (There is a Pybus Street somewhere off Ashbourne Road, or Pubys Street, as it is rather engagingly renamed on a local street map.) Everybody talked to Pybus, whether he delivered their milk or not, and after he was retired, he went to live on a farm at Kedleston, at the back of what is now the Kedleston Hotel. Local children, including myself, often used to visit him, and he always remembered us.

The Co-op also had a horse-drawn bread van, a very strange, tall, wooden vehicle, a bit like a prairie schooner, which seemed to be made entirely of wood and made a curious rumbling sound as it progressed round the streets. You could hear it coming from some distance away. I seem to remember it being pulled by a large brown horse, but the whole arrangement was replaced by a van when I was still quite small. Breweries still tended to deliver beer by horse and dray, and I was thrilled to see the beautiful shire horses which pulled them. Apart from Pybus, the most memorable of my horse friends was Dinah, the shire horse who lived in the field off Allestree Lane which I either passed or walked through on my way to school. If I walked along the Lane, Dinah was usually waiting under the hornbeam tree, and if she wasn't, would come ambling across to say hello. I was probably late on quite a few occasions due to waiting to greet Dinah, and would reward her with a stroke of her velvety nose. She seemed to be more of a pet than a working horse, and belonged to Mr Moors, another dark, wild-looking farmer whose farm was next to our school. We always referred to him as Old Moore, as in *Old Moore's Almanac*, but in fact he wasn't all that old, and his name was actually Moors, not Moore. We were all scared stiff of him, on account of his unkempt, shaggy appearance, not to mention his herd of particularly loose-bowelled cows which bespattered the pavement twice daily between field and school. However, like Dinah, he was probably a gentle soul at heart.

There were not many other tradespeople around, apart from a slightly odd young woman known simply as the Egg Girl, who would bring round eggs in a basket and sometimes drove a small, dilapidated van, accompanied by a rather dim kid named Raymond. She seemed a faintly pathetic character and someone once told me in confidence that her husband abused her, which would certainly explain the nasty bruise I remember once seeing on her forehead. That sort of thing was seldom heard of, or at least spoken about, in those days, and everyone tended to feel a bit sorry for her. The poultry farm was somewhere on the far side of the Lane, and, like the fields on our side, was eventually built on.

Gradually, by the time I was ten, building work had begun on the land between our house and the school, which until then had only been marked out by a line of kerbstones in a few places, which petered out into nothing. All building work had ceased in 1939, five years before I was born, and our own road had large gaps in it, the road itself being unfinished from just below our own house. The pavement was again simply marked with a line of kerbstones and, like the road, consisted mainly of clinker and stone. On looking at old photos, mostly taken around the time I was born, I am amazed how basic and run-down the local streets looked in those years after the War. Most houses were painted green, the only colour of paint that seemed to be available apart from black, yet somehow they lacked the dull uniformity they have now. They all had front gardens, even if some were a bit overgrown, and most had fences and gates. Only a few had garages and hardly anyone had a car. Before the War, my parents had owned a small car, but, left outside in the awful winters they had then, untended and ultimately without petrol, it deteriorated so badly it ended up in the scrapyard.

But things were changing. For quite a few more years, though, you could still walk through the ridge-ploughed fields between the top of our road and the school, at least until I was in my teens. They were beautiful fields, always studded with buttercups and daisies. Wild roses grew in the hedgerows, with stitchwort, celandines, violets and cuckoo-flowers beneath. Sometimes they were just filled with mowing grass which rippled when the wind blew and cloud shadows scudded across them. When I read Dylan Thomas's line *fire green as grass*, I knew exactly what he meant.

The path we followed, reputed to be part of the Roman road which led from Little Chester across Darley Grove, ultimately crossed towards Kedleston and Mackworth and linked up with Long Lane, the far side of Kirk Langley. Parts of it are still there. At the bottom corner of the field, near the Allestree Lane end, was a pond, where Dinah would often be found. This was partly fed by a shallow stream which ran along Allestree Lane, and was reputedly not drained when the new houses were built there until the occupants discovered water running under their floorboards.

Woodlands Road, which met the Lane on the corner, was part of a development of council houses which seem to have been begun around the time the school was built, just in time for me to start there after Easter in 1949. We were told that the road had once been lined by a beautiful avenue of beech trees which were felled during the Second World War, much to everyone's horror. It seems possible, though, that the wood may have been used to make aircraft. I believe the de Havilland Mosquito was made of wood, so that could have been an explanation. Land at the top of Woodlands Road and Woodlands Lane was taken over by the War Department and used for tank trials, as was part of Burley Hill. One farm, on the corner of Woodlands Lane, known as Jepson's Farm, was requisitioned by them and its owner forced to leave. According to my grandmother, who knew him, he never really recovered and the farm was still derelict for many years after the War. There were Nissen huts over Jonty Farmers, and both the local parks were used by the military. Everything then had that strange air of impermanence, and although children of my own age knew next to nothing of the War, since our parents preferred not to talk about it, it was always there in the background, as I said before, an unseen bogeyman, a shadow, a word.

By the time I was eight or nine, a few new houses had already filled in the gaps in our street, and to my horror, I learned that one of them was to be occupied by our not entirely popular headmistress. Miss J, with whom my parents had clashed as politely as possible over such incidents as illness and school holidays (how little things change), was a large, booming-voiced lady with a massive bosom on which was often pinned, like a flag on a golf course, a curious felt daffodil. However, once she had established herself, my friends and I soon discovered, to our great delight, from the footpath at the top of the road, the edifying sight of Miss J's enormous bloomers trembling on the washing line.

EIGHT

Schooldays

The new school at Allestree was opened at just the right time for me, luckily. Hitherto, the only choice had been the village school, which was singularly unpopular and had a bad name for bullying teachers. One of my cousins and several of their friends had been so badly treated there that at least one of them had to be taken away, though where they were sent, I'm not quite sure, as I was too young to be told about this at the time. Presumably, this was why my mother was determined that I shouldn't be sent there, and I remember going with her to have a look at the convent school in town. This seemed rather dark and depressing – and were the nuns any gentler, one wondered? However, I was never to find out, as the new County Primary School on Robincroft Road opened just in time for me to start there after Easter 1949.

The school was housed in a collection of prefabricated buildings, which, I was only told recently, the village schoolchildren referred to as The Cowshed, and these were supposed to be only temporary. However, they were still there over twenty years later and not fully replaced for thirty or so. But they were light and clean, and just fine as far as we were concerned. My first teacher was a Mrs Fisher, grey-haired and kindly. On my first day, I was put in the tender care of a girl I knew slightly, pretty but vicious, who lived quite near. She pinched me very hard on my bare arm, so I hit her with my blue plastic handbag. It had a metal clasp, which was unfortunate, as it obviously hurt and she howled, but luckily no one heard. I can't remember much about that first school year, except that there was a Wendy house in the classroom and if we were good, we could drink our milk in there. I hated milk, which made me feel sick, so I was excused the free school milk which was supposed to be so good for us, along with the National Health orange juice, which made me *violently* sick (so much for good intentions), so presumably, even if I was very good, my times in the Wendy house were probably few. There were other compensations. In the field at the back was an interesting tree stump, shaped like a chicken, rubbed smooth by the climbing and sliding of many children, which must have been used by them long before the school opened. Mum said the tree was a sycamore. I'm not sure how she knew. It was there for many years after I left. There was a playground covered with asphalt in the front, too, but we much preferred the field.

Next to the field was an orchard, which must have been originally part of Mr Moors' orchard which lay next door, divided from it by a wire fence, and still had quite a few fruit trees. If we found an apple or a pear (and I still find this hilarious), we were supposed to retrieve it carefully and hand it in to the cooks in the school kitchen. Since the cooks were a large, fierce, red-elbowed lot, if I ever found anything, I'd prefer to leave it to rot rather than hand it in to them, since they always looked as though they'd probably belt any passing child and chuck them into the nearest boiling pot. Since my mother was at home all day and we lived not far away, I did not normally have school dinners anyway, for which I was deeply grateful. The only times I was obliged to have one, due to some minor family crisis (which caused Miss J, the headmistress, no end of stress and another exchange of grumpy notes), they were depressingly awful.

Our next teacher was Mrs Hall, who was dark and good-looking and wore interesting colour combinations. I especially remember a deep yellow suit, with a matching string of large, glossy yellow beads. After her came Mr Bishop, who was young and very entertaining, in a droll kind of way. I really liked him. Both were good teachers and my time with them was happy. Then, after that, the dreaded Mr Smyth from Belfast, whose temper was short and whose English incomprehensible. Mr Smyth, too, was short, and had possibly just come out of the army, as he shouted and raved at the children like a demented sergeant major in a *Carry On* film. I dare say quite a few teachers had recently been in the armed forces, including Miss Barnes, who took over the infants class after Mrs Fisher. Her stentorian bellowing could be heard for several miles, although I was told she was actually quite tame. All the same, I was relieved she didn't teach me.

Prior to my year with Mr Smyth, I had just about sussed out the idea of maths, courtesy of my dad and Mr Bishop, and although it was clear I'd never be much good at it, I could just about cope. However, after a few weeks with Mr Smyth, any progress was promptly reversed and never regained. Luckily, I was very good at English (unlike Mr Smyth) and art, and about that time, Miss Birch joined the school. There were actually two Miss Birches, both quite young and attractive; Miss Freda, the older one, and her sister, Miss Lamorna, who joined the school about a year later. Neither of them was ever my class teacher, but Miss Lamorna did teach us art, for which I was grateful, as she was particularly nice to me. We always assumed they were the daughters of Lamorna Birch the painter, though I've never been able to confirm this. They were not at all alike. Recent research showed that Lamorna Birch the artist did have a daughter who was known as Mornie, but the dates didn't seem to tally with our Miss Lamorna. Miss Freda was shorter, with light auburn hair, and wore noticeable make-up, whereas Miss Lamorna, who didn't seem to use make-up, was tall and dark, with long flowing hair, very much the traditional bohemian, I suppose. She was also kind and unaffected. When I left to go to grammar school, Miss Lamorna was the only other teacher, apart from our class teacher, to whom I gave a gift, and I remember that she seemed genuinely pleased.

The top class was taught by Mrs Rose, a rather strict lady who, at the time, lived quite near to us, on the road taken when the field path was impassable. I was always a little in awe of her, as she seemed a bit humourless and aloof, showing little interest in children other than those in her own class. Once they left, she severed all interest again. Despite this, she was a very good teacher and prepared us well for the Eleven Plus and the years that followed. However, of all the teachers I encountered at both junior and senior schools, there were only a handful who actively encouraged me and showed any genuine interest in what skills I had, and Miss Lamorna was one of them.

Miss J, our aforementioned headmistress, was another kettle of fish entirely, and a pretty hefty kettle at that. Perhaps more of a boiler, really, but let's not get personal. Miss J tended to show an interest in two classes of people only: the rich, to whom she bowed and scraped and fawned in an ingratiating manner, and the poor, whom she patronised to an embarrassing degree. Anyone who came somewhere in the middle (like, for instance, me, and, if it comes to that, most of us) didn't really exist for her, or was, at least, beneath her contempt. To be fair to Miss J, she seemed much pleasanter in my earlier days at the school, although, as my mother was once unwise enough to comment, if only in a jovial manner, a little overambitious and publicity conscious. This remark, alas, was clearly reported back to Miss J, who, thereafter, had us in her bad books. However, at some time during my time at the school, there was a serious health scare, and although I was lucky enough not to be affected, an awful lot of children were, and Miss J was held responsible. This must have been a great embarrassment to her, and it seemed to be after this that she became so vindictive and unpleasant.

My favourite Miss J anecdote concerns a small boy, and I can't remember who he was, but he clearly knew on which side his bread was buttered. As the dear lady prepared to leave our classroom, said small boy hurled himself towards the door in front of her, leading to the following verbatim exchange:

Miss J: How *dare* you push in front of me, you *wretched* little boy!

Small Boy: But I was only going to open the door for you, Miss.J.

Which turned him on the spot from Smarmy Little Git to Local Hero. Still can't remember who he was, though.

One of Miss J's reluctant pets was a very nice but sadly not awfully bright kid who had rich parents. We'll call him Harry. He tolerated Miss J's fawning with embarrassed dignity as she informed all and sundry, especially his parents, who she clearly hoped would present the school with some valuable trophy or maybe a fully equipped gymnasium, what a genius he was and how well he would do. Harry's mother (I never met his father) was a large, florid lady, apt to wear dazzling white and much jewellery, who reminded me of Mrs Williams in Dylan Thomas's story *The Peaches* the moment I read it. Harry suffered her with patient resignation. He also suffered from what is nowadays sometimes referred to as 'clumsy child syndrome' and could always be relied upon to trip over a mat or knock over a vase or a music stand, preferably at the most inappropriate moment possible. This he would brush off with one of his endearing teddy-bear grins and a cheerful "Whoops!" while Miss J looked the other way. One day, during a Scripture class when we were talking about the Jews, he stood up and said, in his deep, gruff voice, "Please, miss, I'm a Jew", and promptly sat down again. We were all very impressed. Indeed, I still am. Everybody liked Harry. Not because he was rich, but simply because he was nice. Much to Miss J's undoubted annoyance, he failed his scholarship and was probably ferried off to some expensive private school to create happy chaos elsewhere. I often wonder what happened to him. I hope life was kind. "You can't make a silk purse out of a sow's ear, Mrs—," Miss J is reputed to have told someone's mother at a parents' evening. (Not a rich parent, presumably.) One assumes that after he got his PhD she recanted those words. Or perhaps not. Well, you can do anything with a sow's ear these days...

Mr Smyth, of dreaded reputation, once told a girl I knew that she was "mentally deficient and should be locked up". I'm not sure what she had done to deserve this heart-warming accolade. Teachers in those days were often physically violent, and it was nothing to give a child a quick clout round the head or a sharp whack across the hand with a ruler. Objects were thrown, and books and even shoes used as weapons. While I personally am not opposed to the occasional light smack where and when required, the use of such violence as we saw is definitely not to be recommended, and it was apparently much worse in our parents' and grandparents' day. Enough said! On looking at my old school reports, I realise I spent two horrendous years with Sir Smyth, during which my marks deteriorated considerably.

One of the worst aspects of Mr Smyth's class was that hardly anybody could understand what he was saying. It never seemed to occur to anyone that this might be the reason why quite a few children stayed in his class longer than usual before going on to the top class because they had made so little progress. It was some weeks before I learned the meaning of one particular instruction which consisted of several short, sharp barks and a snarl. I finally translated this by peering from under the cover of my desk lid to see what other children were doing. It was "Take out your rough work books."

There was a particular girl I would sit with occasionally who used to come and go during my time at the school. She was dark and pretty and wore a bangle of plaited straw and possibly (unless I imagined this) tiny gold hoop earrings. It has since occurred to me that her family might have been Travellers. Her name was either Linda or Anna and we were quite friendly. One day, during one of her sporadic appearances, she was sitting next to me gazing abstractedly out of the window when Sir Smyth came and rapped on the desk and asked her severely what the whatever she thought she was doing. "Just watching this little bird out of the window, sir," came the unabashed reply. Even Sir Smyth was lost for words. I was told later that he was actually fond of birds. So maybe he did have a softer side after all.

The trouble with living in a place like Derby was that, because of the amount of work available at the time, with Rolls-Royce and the railway etc., it was always a bit of a transit camp, with families coming and going. Although my own family stayed put – my dad's family had moved here from rural areas to work on the railway not far away a century earlier – many of my friends' families soon moved on and I lost touch with them. Sally, Simon and his brother, and of course my best friend Pauline, had all gone within the space of a few years. There was Margaret, with whom I played a great deal, wandering the half-built streets together, playing games re-enacted from the stories she told derived from films seen by her numerous relatives; Margot, whose eccentric widowed mother kept a boarding house and lived on the edge of town; Linda, who came and went; and one or two others, though no one ever quite made up for the loss of Pauline.

Later, when we went on to secondary school, all of us were put into different classes and eventually regrouped entirely. We were a mixed bag, then, not seemingly divided by wealth or class, since, as Muriel Spark begins, in *The Girls of Slender Means*, '*Long ago in 1945 all the nice people in England were poor...*' So were many of the nasty ones, as well. It was not really until the mid '50s that things began to change. The War had been a great leveller, and I never felt Derby itself was a class-conscious place. We suburbanites, the village children, the council house children, the posher children from the big houses on Duffield Road, Linda who came and went, the children from the prefabs and old railway carriages by the brook – we all played together and nobody bothered. It was well into the '50s – was it after the coronation, perhaps? – that snobbishness and superiority started to return and those stupid, pointless divisions began all over again.

NINE

The Phantom Plane, Gremlins, Brownies and Books

One day, as I was coming home from the shops, accompanied by Margaret, for some reason we were both in a bad mood. Whether this was due to our recent eleven-plus tests or just because we'd been told off for messing up the comics outside the paper shop again, I can't remember, but as we got part way up Hollies Road, near the entrance to what is now Sycamore Avenue, still in the process of being built, we heard a plane approaching. Margaret looked up (and this is one of those 'Be careful what you wish for' moments) and muttered, "I hope it crashes." The sound of engines grew louder, and as we looked up between the houses, to our horror, we saw what seemed to be a large four-engined aircraft with a glass dome over the cockpit flying very low, as if in trouble. The glass dome was smashed and the propellers seemed to be turning slower and slower. As it struggled over us and disappeared over the houses opposite, we stood frozen in horror as we waited for the crash. Nothing happened. Total silence. It had completely disappeared. No plane. No sound. No smoke. Nothing. It had simply gone.

While I was writing this (30th March 2018), a number of people claimed to have sighted several apparently old aircraft over the areas of Ripley and Heage not far away, which were flying very low and seemed strange. However, the RAF responded the following day that the planes were three RAF Hercules from Brize Norton on a training exercise. But what appear to have been phantom wartime aircraft *have* been sighted many times in Derbyshire, usually in the Peak District. Generally, the plane in question would seem about to crash, which of course, quite a few did. And early one evening in 1981, together with my three daughters, I myself was a witness to what seemed to be a Lancaster bomber flying very low over Mickleover, when one *was* not, and indeed *could* not have been, actually there. Completely fascinated, we watched it pass over our house and disappear behind the houses opposite.

There were, I believe, converted Lancasters and a few other wartime aircraft used as freight carriers, and some for passengers, still around in the 1950s. So what did my friend and I actually see in 1955? Could it have been some sort of hallucination? Did we imagine the smashed dome and the slowing propellers? I honestly don't know. It may be that what people see, or think they see, is some form of action replay of the past, something that has imprinted itself upon the landscape through the sheer fear of those who experienced it. The plane my daughters and I saw in 1981 certainly seemed like a replay of the past, although it didn't look as though it was about to crash – in fact it was flying steadily and seemed perfectly normal, except that it showed no lights of any kind. The former wartime airfield of Shaw-wood near Ashbourne would have been only a few miles away. Someone my daughter met ten years later believed she and her grandmother had seen it too, around the same time, though there doesn't seem to be a record of it being seen by anyone else. No restored Lancasters were operational at the time. There was no rational explanation. But 1955? I keep an open mind.

With Margaret, I became a member, for about a year, of the Brownie pack in Darley Abbey, which seemed to be the nearest, as Allestree had Girl Guides but not Brownies. Perhaps someone thought it would be good for us. However, on the whole, we found it pretty boring and rather twee. At its best, it was unimaginative, and the most enjoyable bit was the bus journey there and back, followed by the long, dark walk from the village to our homes. I doubt you'd let your under-tens do this nowadays. The meetings were in the old school in Darley Village, which was a pretty depressing building in itself, dark and dismal, close to the entrance to Darley Park. On one side of the road was the village lock-up, a small round or conical building which was knocked down shortly afterwards, and the bus stop was by a tumbledown stone wall full of holes, with a sloping field behind it. There may have been one miserly street lamp some distance away, but everywhere was pitch black. As far as I recall, we would catch a bus from Allestree Lane on the way there, but there wasn't one on the way back, and we had to walk from Allestree village, about a mile or so, still dark as we approached our school and Mr Moors' farm, which had a massive black overhang of ivy shadowing the road, and if we were very lucky, an owl would hurtle out and scare the hell out of us. We loved that.

We were accompanied on these expeditions by a girl from the Lane and a younger child, who she insisted was her niece. Little smarty-pants that I was, I told her she couldn't be an auntie till she was grown up, so she must be her cousin. It was ages before someone enlightened me. This girl, like Margot from the guest house, was the youngest of a large family and had siblings who were adults before she was born. But I couldn't quite grasp the concept of that. Her parents were elderly and (like so many of our locals) definitely a bit eccentric, and she always seemed slightly neglected somehow, but she was a nice girl and we all four enjoyed our long, dark walks together much more than we enjoyed the actual Brownies sessions, which were painstakingly slow, though I did learn how to sew buttons on. Eventually, having realised that it would take until I was about fifty before I graduated to become a Girl Guide, I gave up and left, and I suppose the others must have done too. What I wanted then was something more imaginative, more stimulating...

My parents both read a lot, if not necessarily intellectual stuff, but I was always encouraged to read, which I loved. There weren't many new books around when I was small, as few were published in the War years and what there were in the way of children's books tended to be reprints on poor-quality paper, so much of the stuff I read was second-hand. My parents often read to me, before and after I was old enough to read for myself, and I enjoyed the usual children's books of the time, such as Beatrix Potter, and Alison Uttley's *Little Grey Rabbit* books, some of which I still have, as well as *Sam Pig*, although most of my early books seem to have disappeared; probably fallen to bits or given away. I was delighted to learn that the latter were set in Derbyshire, though, and also only learned recently that the illustrator of most of the early Ladybird Books, which I also had, were done by a Derby artist, as well as being printed in Loughborough, not far away. I also liked Cicely Mary Barker's *Flower Fairies* books, which, like Beatrix Potter and the *Little Grey Rabbit* books with their lovely Margaret Tempest illustrations, were artistically very attractive.

I recently found a copy of A. A. Milne's *When We Were Very Young*, though I don't seem to have had any Winnie-the-Pooh books of my own. *When We Were Very Young* was given to me by some friends – railway people, old family friends of my parents, who moved away – and is dated Xmas 1950. They had lived in a house quite near the bus stop where we used to wait after Brownies, and had two daughters, so I suspect they may have moved before then, as I never remember seeing them during this time. We used to go to their house for tea sometimes, and their mother, Auntie A, was memorable for her somewhat unusual 'trifles' which tended to consist of the week's supply of pudding leftovers soaked in cold custard and finished off by having a tin of evaporated milk thrown over them to the cry of "Cream, anyone?" as a sort of last rite, before you could shout, "No!" Despite this, we stayed the best of friends for many years! Their eldest daughter, the same age as me, was great fun. And it was in their house that I ate my very first Marmite sandwich…

Other books I liked, as I got older and was reading more for myself, were the *Jane* books by Evadne Price. These were written over a period of time between the Wars and into the early 1950s, almost parallel with Richmal Crompton's *William* books, which I also read, but for my money were more entertaining. Jane was slightly more of an anarchist than William and I always felt the humour in later William books was a bit laboured, although I enjoyed both. But of course, Jane was a girl as well as naughty, which added much to the charm of the stories. There were also only about ten of them, so they didn't get stale, but I never managed to get my hands on more than three or four, as they went out of print. I also loved a book called *Nancy and Plum* by Betty MacDonald, about two American orphans. MacDonald also wrote *The Egg and I*, which was aimed at adults, though I remember reading that too.

A little later, I read many of Enid Blyton's school stories, as well as those about the Chalet School by Elinor Brent-Dyer, all of which gave a rather romanticised picture of life at fancy boarding schools, but the only person I knew who'd actually been to one was my cousin Tessa, who'd got some kind of grant and gone to the same school in Darley Dale, quite coincidentally, where Richmal Crompton had been both a pupil and a teacher. Like most children of my generation, I read loads of Enid Blyton, which I don't think did me any harm.

Malcolm Saville was another author I liked, and Arthur Ransome – well, at least a proportion of his stuff. Some of it was a little too hearty for my taste. I wonder how many people know that this author of upper-middle-class children's fiction was an enthusiastic Bolshevik who was married to Trotsky's secretary?

The first library I remember, and where I discovered the *Jane* books, was the old Railway Institute Library opposite Derby Midland Station. The County Libraries were few and far between then, and Allestree didn't yet have one. Since we didn't live in the Borough of Derby, we probably weren't entitled to use the town library. Boots (the chemist) had a library of sorts – in fact my eldest cousin, who married the farmer, worked there before she took on the onerous duties of a farmer's wife – but I don't think they stocked children's books and I don't remember going there. The local paper shop also loaned out a few books, but it was the Railway Institute Library that I remember best. It was rather dark with tall shelves bulging with books, most of which were old and pretty dirty – so dirty and well used, in fact, that the staff used to put blue paper covers on them before they issued them – but it was magic. The lighting was very yellow, and I wonder if it might have been gas lighting, but it was somehow fuggy and cosy and I loved it. I didn't go there all that often, as my dad usually got books for me on his way home, but just occasionally I would meet him there. All those kinds of establishments, like the Mechanics Institutes too (Charles Dickens himself did readings at Derby Mechanics Institute), had been set up in Victorian times, intended for the education, as well as relaxation, of working people, but most of them are restaurants, private clubs or simply drinking dens now. Sadly, the education bit seems to have gone out of the window. Never mind, we've got the Internet...

Most of the characters in the books I read then were, of course, rather upper or upper middle class, and usually had maids, cooks and nannies (heavens!), although, I have to admit, in the years between the Wars, or so I was told, both sets of grandparents did, for a time, have a maid or two, though presumably not when they were living in the terraced house in Chester Green. I remember seeing a play at the Playhouse Studio in Derby in the 1980s called *The Golden Pathway Annual*, in which children from the present met some of their childhood heroes from those books and found they were too posh to speak to them. Ah, yes. As an aside, I did have a very distant relative called Deirdre (and in those pre-*Coronation Street* days, you needed pretty high aspirations before you named your daughter Deirdre), and found the same applied. I had often admired her elegant silver-framed photo on Gran's sideboard, but alas, on our one and only meeting, Deirdre merely dimpled demurely and hid behind the nearest adult. "She's very shy," said adult remarked hastily, by way of compensation, but I knew where I stood. I hadn't discovered Arthur Ransome's left-wing leanings at the time.

One of the things I did notice about the books I read was that most of them were set in the fairly recent past – that's to say, before the Second World War – and I was always intrigued by the illustrations, especially the clothes and haircuts, which seemed a world away from what we were wearing by the time I was reading them. Another thing that seemed strange was the reference to food, and how much of it there seemed to be in those days – I remember being horrified when a character in an Enid Blyton story actually *threw away* a ham sandwich – this was unheard of! Ham, when I was growing up, was a thing of luxury in those days of food rationing, even if dry and curled up – but *throwing it away*? Who *did* that? Gosh, they were privileged in those far-off days! Whatever happened to the 'Hungry '30s'? We were never told about those. Not in books, anyway. But we were not allowed to waste food, though, even after rationing had ended, and to this day, I never do. No, as far as children were concerned, social issues and things like poverty were tactfully avoided.

I did discover American and Canadian classics such as *What Katy Did* and *Anne of Green Gables* (though both, of course, dated from the past), and the aforementioned more contemporary *Nancy and Plum*, in which the characters appeared a little more equal, but it seemed a long time before modern British children's books caught up with them, on the social scale, at least. On the other hand, re *The Egg and I*, this did not necessarily apply to American books written for adults, and I do remember certain aspects of it – and one or two other books, too – making me feel somewhat uncomfortable. Casual classism and racism seemed to be thought of as more or less acceptable then, on both sides of the Atlantic. Well, not to me it wasn't, anyway. Nor was the fact that in most books, it tended to be the boys, rather than the girls, who had the most fun. Girls had a tendency to be a bit wimpish. Apart from Jane.

The County Library at Allestree eventually opened at the side of our school, probably about the time I was due to leave it, in a white-painted wooden building, entered via some steps. It was operated by the rather glamorous and (obviously, for Allestree) slightly eccentric Joan, accompanied by a small dog called Susie. "A very *naughty* dog," she told me, last time I spoke to her, a few years ago. This was before the dogs ban, which came into operation some fifteen years or so later, when I was working in the library service myself, much to the disgruntlement of a very large police dog named Ranger, who thereafter lay diagonally across the doorstep, thus effectively preventing anyone from coming in or out until PC Doghandler (I've forgotten his name, but he was more approachable than Ranger) had finished choosing his books. It gave us a nice quiet half-hour, though. This wooden library eventually burned down and the library was rehoused in the old lodge gatehouse at the top of Main Avenue near Allestree Park, which also duly burned down. Perhaps someone was trying to tell us something. I have a feeling the one beside the school was rebuilt, before being ultimately relocated to a new building at Park Farm, the housing estate which now covers Jonty Farmers, rather to the annoyance of locals, who then had much further to walk to get there. But of course, everyone in Allestree, deemed 'posh', was expected to have a car. Not necessarily so, as it happened.

TEN

The Big Houses, and the Ones We Didn't Inherit

Allestree Park was about a mile from our house, so not often visited until I was a bit older and could go on my own, and it was not a formal park, but mostly woodland, with a golf course on one side, a large grassy area and a deep natural lake at the bottom. One of the more entertaining aspects of walking there in the evening was the guy who used to row himself into the middle of the lake in a small boat, drop anchor, and lie flat on his back playing the trombone. Where, presumably, no one could get at him. (It may well have been a trumpet. I forget. Whichever is the more likely instrument for playing while flat on one's back, presumably.) I never found out who he was, or how long he continued to do this before somebody either sabotaged his boat or shot him.

Allestree Hall, ironically, is the only one of the three main large houses remaining in the Derby parks – Allestree, Darley

Abbey and Markeaton, all of which were not planned public parks but originally private estates. I say 'ironically' since it is undoubtedly the ugliest and least desirable as a residence. It's still unoccupied in 2019, and has been as long as I can remember, although it has been through a number of different incarnations and partial uses as flats and offices etc., but no one ever seemed to stay very long. Markeaton Hall, as already mentioned, was trashed by troops and finally neglected until demolition seemed to be the only option, while Darley was used as a school, and survived (just about) a couple of fires, until the latter also applied. Allestree Hall has always been a grim-looking pile and, as a child, I found it slightly frightening. The woods were quite scary too, as parts of them are very dense and deep indeed, and only recently, with some family members, I managed to get lost in them.

Chaddesden, too, once had a hall, which bit the dust in the late 1920s, when, as so often happened then, the family who owned it found it too expensive to maintain and demolished it, though the park remains. Osmaston Hall (which was in Osmaston by Derby, not Osmaston near Ashbourne) met the same fate and most of it eventually disappeared under Ascot Drive Industrial Estate, though the odd little church of St James the Less (aptly named, as it happened) survived, intimidated by later industrial buildings till fairly recently. Osmaston Manor near Ashbourne, which had a famous polo ground, lasted until the 1960s before it, too, was consigned to rubble, though the parkland and a curious tower, once part of a heating system, remain. And Elvaston Castle, with its strange trees and spooky rock adornments, well outside the city limits, is still in existence as a bone of contention for the local authorities though currently a popular place for walking. I don't remember ever going that far afield as a child, however. My grandfather told me a strange story about Osmaston

Manor, dating, I think, from when he was young, probably before the turn of the last century, saying that a man who was working in the grounds with a horse and cart was simply swallowed up by the earth one day, horse, cart and all, and never recovered. I was always intrigued by this. Presumably some kind of subsidence was responsible, as the landscape there is damp and hilly with some very steep slopes, but I'd love to know more about the story.

Grandpa was a great source of strange information, and told us a family member had once lived in a house near Yoxall in Staffordshire called Sherholt Lodge, which he claimed was haunted. He often stayed there as a child and said the walls of his room used to glow at night, and when they renovated it, bones and human skulls were found which they believed dated to an incident in the English Civil War, and had been shovelled behind the panelling, packed in earth. I tried to research this in the 1990s, though never managed to visit the house, and the lady who lived there wrote back that she did know a little about the rumours of haunting but couldn't really go into it, and we were not able to pursue it further. I never found the name of the relative who had lived there, unfortunately, and the occupant in the 1990s told me it had been in her husband's family for many generations. None of the names seemed to tally, so I guessed Grandpa's relative had been connected through the female line and had married into theirs, probably being one of the Holbrook or Antill families on his mother's side.

The Antills owned The Homestead, a wonderful Georgian house in Spondon, and my third great-grandmother, Sarah Antill, seems to have lived there before her marriage, but again, being on the female side, none of this grandiose stuff passed down to me! Anyhow, when I heard these stories from

Grandpa, I knew nothing of the Antills and very little about the Holbrooks, other than a vague story that a Miss Antill (whose name at that stage I didn't know) had 'married beneath her' and it hadn't gone down very well with her family. I do have two inherited embroideries, though, which may have been done by her, though the valuer I asked about them thought they were earlier, so could have been done by her mother. Herbert Spencer, the Derby-born philosopher, was also an in-law, and a friend of my great-grandmother, who would have been Sarah Antill's daughter, as he had grown up with her father, William Holbrook.

My great-grandmother, Lizzie, was often visited by Herbert Spencer when he came back to Derby, and they were living around the Osmaston Road and Sacheverel Street area, as his family had also moved to the same part of Derby. I still have a small pewter jug which he gave her. The story, according to Grandpa, was that Lizzie once asked Herbert to fetch her a pound of butter, but, being an absent-minded sort, he forgot what she'd asked him for, so presented her with the jug instead, "because he thought she'd like it better". Herbert's actual birthplace, in Exeter Street, was thoughtlessly torn down around 1970 to be replaced by a car wash. There was originally a blue plaque over the door, which I did manage to photograph in situ shortly before the house was destroyed. There is a bas-relief plaque on nearby Exeter Bridge commemorating him.

Lizzie Holbrook, who married my great-grandfather, Charles Neal, died not long before I was born. According to my mother, Lizzie had a number of well-to-do relatives, some of whom lived at either Burnaston House or Burnaston Hall, I am not clear which, but possibly the large house which was taken down before the Toyota factory was built on the old Derby Airport site and is still in pieces awaiting resurrection. I've never been able to establish who these relatives were, either, but suspect they were all aunts from the Antill side of the family who had 'married well', as they used to say in those days, since Lizzie's father was simply a butcher, but he did own more than one shop, so probably wasn't short of a bob or two. The Holbrooks seem to have started off as farmers and graziers and worked their way up in society. Lizzie was very upright in her younger days (she certainly looks strict in the only photograph I have of her), and her sons described her, rather unsympathetically, as "a bit of a termagant." I think nowadays, 'formidable' would be a more probable term to use. In later years, she must have mellowed a lot, since to my mother and her brothers, she was very much the kindly grandma.

ELEVEN

The Neals

Grandpa's own family, the Neals, had come from Lincolnshire, and, so he told us, lived in a village called Wootton, from whence his father had been sent as a servant to work at a big house, after his own father went off to the American Civil War. The name Neal, spelled with or without a final 'e', is of Scandinavian origin, and extremely common in Lincolnshire. I have found both my great-great-grandfather, William, and my great-great-grandmother, Ann Dinnis, on the 1851 census at Hessle in South Yorkshire, working as servants in a country house before their marriage. I've never been able to verify the details of the Civil War part of the story, since quite a few William Neals seem to have fought on both sides, but I have learned recently that over twenty thousand Englishmen went to support the Northern cause, as allegedly did my great-grandfather's father. He was presumed killed, and his eldest son – Charles, my great-grandfather – ran away aged about twelve or thirteen, after being ill-treated at another big house where he worked as a pantry boy, sleeping in ditches in a freezing winter, surviving on wild plants and mangolds put out for the cattle, and ending up first in Nottingham and then in Derby, where he found work at a grocery warehouse owned by a Mr Morley. He stayed there for the rest of his life, becoming a partner in the business, and married Lizzie Holbrook. He died in 1930. Neal & Morley were still operational until the late 1950s, when Charles's son, my grandfather, died.

I've never been able to verify the whole of Charles's story either, but certainly some of it is true, though not all the dates and ages seem to tally. Clearly my great-grandfather's family had fallen on hard times and had worked as servants in big houses, but who exactly had done what and gone where has been hard to establish. The approximate date of William's disappearance from the UK census certainly ties in with the Civil War. By the 1861 census, only the mother and children are left, though the mother is still described as 'married', and by 1871 the children are all dispersed and the mother gone. Since a UK census is only taken every ten years, one can only speculate as to what happened in between. By 1881, Charles is in Derby. I only wish my grandfather had lived long enough to tell me more.

Neal & Morley and Our Warehouse

(The following is taken from a piece I wrote ten years ago, now enlarged and slightly edited, about our fascinating warehouse in Bloom Street, inaccessible now, hidden behind a locked metal door beside the former Shelter shop in St Peter's Street.)

I remember Bloom Street. Not many people do. For, even fifty years ago, few people actually lived there. The street itself was hidden, entered by a narrow passage between shops and the half-timbered Cheshire Cheese pub on what was then the busiest shopping street in Derby. The passage was enclosed by buildings, one of which formed its roof, and as dark as pitch. The bricks seemed to glisten slightly, where a hint of light filtered through from the street outside. But the tunnel itself was black, damp and secretive.

Once through the passage, the street opened out, though still narrow and hemmed in by buildings, three storeys on one side, four on the other. Under foot, cobbles, bumpy and worn. At the back of the Cheshire Cheese, its massive wooden doors opening straight onto the street, was our warehouse. Forty years ago, the remaining buildings on Bloom Street were demolished, along with the warehouse, which had already stood empty for a decade. A new shopping centre was built across the end of the street, obliterating all trace of the small Dickensian houses and tangled alleyways, and reducing Bloom Street to an anonymous, truncated yard.

In the 1950s and early '60s, when I was growing up, Derby was a thriving town of dark buildings and tall department stores with gracious Victorian staircases and polished wooden fittings; proper shops with haberdashery and millinery departments full of sculpted hats, costume jewellery and bridal veils. There were modernist blocks with Art Deco curves, small grocery stores and fruiterers, ironmongers, and chemists with pointed bottles of brightly coloured water. Proper shops, with pavements outside and sky up above. Department stores had cosy cafes on their upper floors, from which you could look down on the thronging streets below, and watch, on late winter afternoons, the shops and window displays, headlamps and traffic lights blurring into a kaleidoscope of colours. When it rained, the colours morphed into abstraction as the reflections shone back from the wet pavements.

Bloom Street was near the top of St Peter's Street, close to the area known for decades, inexplicably, as The Spot. Almost opposite was the former family shop, which closed before I was born. As you entered the passage, the hum of traffic shut off as if someone had dropped a switch. Then you entered another world. Bloom Street belonged to the early Victorian world of gas lamps and cobbles, horse-drawn drays and women in pinafores sitting on doorsteps. Our warehouse backed onto the Cheshire Cheese itself, with its rank odour of beer, smoke and sweaty humanity, the sound of men's voices, clinking glasses and the raucous shriek of a barmaid. The warehouse had enormous solid wooden doors that would withstand a siege, with a smaller door cut into them for Grandpa, Uncle Vin, his younger brother, and the staff to come in and out when the main doors were closed. No one knew how old our warehouse was. Just inside the door at the foot of the stairs was Uncle Vin's office. Grandpa's office was at the top of the wooden stairs, which dipped slightly on each tread, worn by the passage of many feet. There was a hole in one step, and on the upper floor, many knotholes from which you could spy on the floor below. A huge wooden pulley like something from a Victorian coal mine was used for hoisting goods from one floor to the other. Above the main doors was a loading bay from which goods could be loaded directly onto the vehicle beneath. Once, while hanging about waiting for my mother, I heard concerned voices talking about an accident. Someone, perhaps one of the lads who worked there, had fallen from those upper doors onto the street and died. Strangely, no one I asked years later remembered this, but ever afterwards in my innermost mind, I saw a man-shaped shadow on the cobbles below.

The warehouse was a magical place, full of nostalgic aromas – coffee, spices, brown sugar, treacle, vinegar and Grandpa' s pipe tobacco. Sides of bacon hung from the ceiling, and there were whole English cheeses wrapped in cheesecloth – round, shiny Dutch ones like footballs in red casing – and enormous tea chests lined with silver foil, full of tea from India, Kenya and Ceylon. At the back was the provisions counter, presided over by Mr Large, pronounced with a soft French 'g' somewhere between a 'j' and a 'z'. I remember him as a big man in a white coat, but his face is a blur. It was Mr Large who weighed out the tea and coffee and sliced the bacon and cheese for the family.

Uncle Vin, the younger Neal brother, looked almost exactly like my grandfather, but was not quite as friendly, or at least, so it seemed, although he was never unpleasant to me. But as a child, I sensed a kind of tension there, something a bit reserved. Later, my mother told me he'd been seriously wounded in the First World War, which had affected him badly. Behind Uncle Vin's office at the foot of the stairs was a shelf with glass jars of brightly coloured sweets and lollipops. These I was not allowed to have, as they were sold to the corner shops in poorer parts of town, presumably Neal & Morley's one concession to inferior merchandise. Perhaps the 'lollipops made from drain water' of urban legend? Certainly I remember Grandpa telling me about a Saturday job when he was a boy in a factory by the river, putting the 'pips' (sawdust splinters) into 'strawberry jam' made of rhubarb. Another urban legend? Maybe! He was always a bit of a joker.

At the back of the warehouse was a narrow yard with a bottle-shaped furnace where packaging and rubbish were burned. You could see it from Grandpa's office window, and beyond it, a similar warehouse backing onto ours, with a furnace in exactly the same place. Beyond that, the grey roofs of terraced cottages, cramped yards, and a grimy red-brick mill. Not far away was the Coliseum Cinema, a beautiful white building with pillars, once a church, where I saw my first Chaplin film with my father, longer ago than I care to remember. If you kept on walking along Bloom Street itself, you finally emerged past some old stock pens via a jitty into Cockpit Hill, opposite the bus station. If you turned left, via another jitty, you would come out somewhere on Albion Street, between the Regal Cinema and the Co-op buildings on East Street.

One day, when I was old enough to go into town on my own, I set out from The Spot towards the warehouse. The town was changing even then, and it was going dark early on a winter afternoon. I scurried down an alleyway, and found myself in a cobbled yard. But the warehouse wasn't there. Smoke was blowing from nearby chimneys and it was getting cold. Dust and ashes blew into my face across empty spaces where demolition had begun. I turned, and suddenly, everything was different. I was lost. Perhaps some familiar landmark had disappeared already to the demolition men's sledgehammers and ball and chain? Surely I was heading towards the bus station and Cockpit Hill? Then I saw the warehouse, its furnace at the back like an HP Sauce bottle, and, with enormous relief, headed towards it. I reached the double doors and stopped, frozen with fright. It wasn't our warehouse at all, but a mirror image of it: wooden doors with a smaller door inside them, cobbled street in front. But no pub, no passage, no name on the door. Panic seized me. I stood staring at a building locked and barred. Every shadow held hidden menace. The darkening sky hung overhead like a sheet of lead. Even the distant burr of traffic had stopped. I turned again. Across the grimy space was another warehouse. At the bottom of the yard, a furnace like an HP Sauce bottle. And from the back, as I looked at it, a dim light showed in a small window on the upper floor. Grandpa's office. Through a fading relief map of streets, picked out only by worn-down kerbs and bits of foundations where the houses had been, I hurried, moving ever faster till I reached Bloom Street.

The town I used to know is no more. The department stores, the outdoor market, the smell of apples and lemons and celery on the cold air of a winter evening are gone. The Art Deco bus station was left to decay till it fell apart. I remember the cheerful mess of Cockpit Hill with its stalls and the oddball characters like Mad Harry who traded there, though I can't remember now what it was he actually sold. The Morledge Market, with its fruit and veg and fabric and pot stalls, had a side entrance onto the bus station. Beyond it were the chip shops and taverns and the shadowy buildings and hidden lives that lay between them and the canal, and the hideous triangular bulk of the Ice Factory, and behind it, the river. I remember the cinemas and corner shops, and streets that once had houses in them. Like Bloom Street and the warehouse, they are just memories now. They were not Venice or Athens, they were not particularly beautiful, but they had character and I miss them.[2]

---

2   Differing versions of this article were published in the *Derby Telegraph* and *Best of British* magazine, for which acknowledgment is given.

TWELVE

The Mysterious Shottons and the Even More Mysterious Whieldons

My Neal grandfather, whose father came from Lincolnshire to seek work, had two sons and one daughter, my mother, their first child, born in 1913, whose earliest memory was of being held up in her father's arms to watch a Zeppelin pass over their house in Normanton to the sound of sirens. Presumably, people at that stage in the First World War were fascinated rather than frightened by the sight of a Zeppelin, though they would be less so shortly afterwards, when one bombed Derby Station. My grandparents lived in Chestnut Avenue when they were first married, which may have been where the Zeppelin incident occurred, then moved to Stenson Road, one of a short row of houses with balconies at the Cavendish, opposite the traffic island. The houses had been built in 1912, just before my grandparents married, and this was the house I always felt to be so creepy. My grandfather worked in his father's business, along with his younger brother, Vincent, but, unlike the much younger Vin, did not have to go to war. On looking at a family photograph taken when my grandfather was about fourteen and Vin about seven, it is heartbreaking to think that this young boy with his bright, eager face would soon be fighting in the trenches. However, although wounded, he survived, and I still have a very sweet postcard he sent to my mother for her birthday from somewhere in France.

My grandmother was born in Quarndon to Thomas F. Shotton, a master tailor, and his strange and fickle wife, Sarah Elizabeth Whieldon, who abandoned her and her two-year-old sister when my grandma was allegedly six days old and set off for a life more adventurous. Grandma's father came from a family, the Shottons, who had also travelled in search of work, and had come from a village in South Staffordshire which is now part of Shropshire, thus making the tracing of family records extremely difficult until one discovers this important fact, since the old handwritten records are often barely legible. Many of the family seem to have been tailors – several, including my great-grandfather, having trained on Savile Row – and this particular branch moved to various places along the Trent Valley before coming to the Derbyshire-Staffordshire border, living for a while on the edge of the Black Country, where my mother remembered being told by her grandfather about the amazing women who worked in the chain workshops, whom he described as "a race of Amazons".

We honestly do not know what hard lives our ancestors lived. Health and Safety rules were non-existent. No work meant no food. After losing a child and becoming ill himself, due to the smoky industrial conditions, my great-grandfather moved his family back to the small community of Barton-under-Needwood, where he had been born and where his two brothers had set up homes. His mother and father were cousins who had married, which had not gone down well with the families. Since so many of the family had the same Christian names as well, it is very difficult to establish who was who. One family lived in Barton and the other in Walton-on-Trent, just inside Derbyshire, while Barton is in Staffordshire. At one time, the brothers and their wives had run the village pub together in Walton, with a tailoring business from the same premises. Everyone seemed to do quite a bit of multitasking in those days. The registration district for both villages was Lichfield.

One brother moved to Burton-on-Trent, where, quite bizarrely, another family of Shottons, whose lives seemed to run parallel with ours, also lived, quite close by. Shotton is not a common name, and while our Shottons came originally from South Staffordshire, the other Shotton enclave is in the North-East of England around Durham, which is where the Burton Shottons had originated. Not only did they have the same surname, but many of their Christian names and ages were also the same, including two daughters called Maude and Florence born around the same time as ours. Their Maude, it was, who came to a singularly bad end, committing suicide after a disastrous honeymoon, and allegedly haunting the already haunted Stapenhill Post Office, which is the curious white-stuccoed building that had always intrigued me when I passed it. (There's a similar one opposite the end of Burton Bridge, originally the Swan Inn; now, I believe, converted into apartments.) After some investigation on Ancestry, I communicated with one of their descendants and we concluded that these two families were not connected at all, but both had equally fascinating histories. Their Florence became a medium. Our Florence had a tragic early death, as did her husband, killed in the Dardanelles, whereas our Maude (my grandmother) had a long life and a very happy marriage. I've often wondered if these two unconnected families knew one another.

Some members of the Shotton family who learned the tailoring trade in London stayed in the South, with one ending up in Reading, while my great-grandfather migrated to Quarndon, a few miles north of Derby, and became the village tailor there. He also wrote a column for the *Derbyshire Advertiser*, did various things on the parish council, was a school governor, an 'overseer for the poor', etc., ran a smallholding and took orders for suits and clothing at Ashbourne Market (as well as betting slips, which seemed to be common practice in those days, thus also giving him the title of 'commission agent'), as well as bringing up two daughters on his own. He was part of a minstrel troupe of some sort which went around putting on shows in village halls. Did he used to black up, I wonder? In those days, this was just thought of as a perfectly acceptable form of entertainment and no offence was intended! It's possible he met his unfortunately ill-matched wife while engaged in amateur theatricals, since she was known to be a good pianist. He was also experienced in dowsing and water-divining, a skill which seems to have been inherited by several family members.

Despite having been abandoned by their mother, my grandmother and her sister seemed to have had a happy childhood and were very fond of their father. We have never established the real circumstances as to how my great-grandmother came to leave them, but there is an odd story which my mother told me which may well have something to do with it. Originally, their home, Vine Cottage, which is on Quarndon Hill almost opposite the little chalybeate well, was thatched, and my great-grandfather decided to have the upper storey raised and a tiled roof put on. One day, while this was going on, my grandmother (born in 1884), then a tiny baby, went missing. According to my mother's version of the story, after a lengthy search, she was found whimpering under a pile of tarpaulins left by the builders and could very well have suffocated. Whether this precipitated my great-grandmother's flight, I don't know – did she abandon the baby and just go, or did she run away because she got the blame for being so careless? Now we will never know. However, another relative's story, which greatly differs and which I'm less inclined to believe, as it seems to have materialised more recently, is that my grandmother had been a toddler and had rolled herself up in a rug, hidden and perhaps fallen asleep before she was found. But I favour the first version, as I'd heard it many times, perhaps originally from Grandma herself!

And what really happened to my errant great-grandmother? The complete story may never be discovered either, but it appears she spent some years travelling the country giving music lessons and earning her living as a pianist before settling with a man in the Potteries, who is described as her 'husband' on one census and with whom she has two children, whom, weirdly, she has named after the two children she abandoned. By the next census, 1901, she is with someone else in another part of the Potteries and has several more children. There is a record of a bigamous marriage to him, describing her as a 'widow' but we know it's her, as she has rather unwisely named the same father (her own), who was, unfortunately, a retired police officer. Her occupation – given, unusually for a woman at this time, on the marriage certificate – is 'pianist'. She's also undergone yet another name change.

Purely by chance – it's amazing what you can discover by just typing someone's name into a search engine – we next come across her in what seems to be an anniversary story that must have been picked out randomly with a pin, since it's from a newspaper in New Zealand, about a woman in Burslem, Stoke-on-Trent, who is claiming maintenance from a husband whom she bigamously married, and who has just discovered her first husband is still alive ("Oh really?" we cry), and has now broken off their relationship. Guess who? Well, well. This is undated, but seems to be about 1906. We next come across her on a transatlantic passenger list with a grown-up daughter and a son of eleven, plus a grandson of three, being 'returned' from Canada in 1914 as 'Charities', presumably meaning they are destitute.

All in all, naughty Sarah Elizabeth clocked up another seven children after leaving her first two, though at least she did take the next two with her when she left 'Husband' Number Two. But there is still a gap of seven years or so after leaving Great-Grandfather Thomas Shotton when we don't know what exactly she was up to, although there were rumours that he had hired a detective to look for her and she'd been sighted playing the piano in a pub somewhere, but that was all. We believe my grandmother knew she was still alive, and letters from the aforementioned private eye were discovered by an uncle searching for something in the Stenson Road attic, but destroyed (by Grandma, presumably) before he could finish examining them. Of course, it was all a massive scandal at the time, especially in a small village like Quarndon, and my great-grandfather and his daughters had to live with it. So did Sarah's father, Thomas Whieldon, the retired police officer, and his family. I have a record of his will from 1915, leaving a sum of money to Sarah on his death in 1917, making it clear that should she predecease him it should pass to her legitimate offspring only. This is worded in some pretty waffly legalese, but it's obvious he had a fair idea of what had been going on. But whether he knew where she was is a different matter. Perhaps this is where the local Sherlock came into it, but that could have been earlier. What happened to the inheritance in the end, I do not know.

Naughty Sarah settled eventually in Tyneside, seemingly after her ignominious return from Canada. Here, according to a distant descendant from one of her less official relationships, she lived in considerable poverty in the shadow of the dockyards. (Did somebody mention Catherine Cookson?) However, only recently, yet another unofficial descendant sent me a photo of her (the only one I've ever knowingly seen) posing by a vintage car which looks to date from the early 1930s, with assorted offspring and possibly 'Husband' Number Three, with whom she seems to have been reconciled. It has a certain 'Bonnie and Clyde' look to it. She finally died in 1950.

Vine Cottage, my grandmother's birthplace, still exists, only slightly altered since she was born there, although it is now divided into three dwellings. I have only been, briefly, into one part of it, the smallest cottage at the end furthest from the road, which a relative of the then-occupant kindly showed me round in the 1990s, when I was studying for my photography degree and working on a piece relating to family photographs. That part of the house, my mother told me, had originally been used as a storeroom, though, and wasn't part of the original dwelling when Grandpa Shotton lived there. When I was a child, a friend of mine from school, whose father later farmed on Cornhill in Allestree, also lived there for a while, and it's possible I may have gone inside briefly to visit someone she knew, but at that time, when I was only seven or eight, I attached less importance to the place. I only wish I'd had the chance to see more of the house proper, but the other occupant seemed to be just a weekender and failed to show up.

According to another lady who had lived there in the past, presumably after my great-grandfather had left in the 1930s, the building had long tailor's tables and high cabinets full of small glass-fronted drawers containing buttons, reels of thread and other sewing items. She also said she thought there had always been some mystery about the place – this may have been to do with the disappearance of Great-Grandmother Sarah, and perhaps of the youngest of my mother's cousins, more of whom later. And Grandma always said the cottage was haunted by a friendly ghost her father called Mrs Huggins, who had a room at the top of the house, the door of which would always stay open, no matter what was put in front of it! As children, they would pile boxes and other items in front of it when they went to bed, and by the morning find they had been moved and the door was open again!

In front of the cottage is now just a truncated yard, but originally this was a lane called Battelle's Lane, which led down to Kedleston Brook at the back of Bath Farm, which was part of what is now the Kedleston Hotel. There was still a passable footpath there some years ago. There was also, to the left of the house, a barn which had been used for a time as a very early Methodist chapel but had been allowed to decay very badly, and when I photographed it in 1993 or '94, it was on its last legs and demolished not very long afterwards. As children, we'd always thought this was the coach house that Grandma had talked about, but the coach house turned out to be an outbuilding attached to the back of the cottage. I never remember Grandma coming to the cottage when I was a child. Perhaps it was too sentimental a journey.

Grandma's sister Florrie was two years older, born when Sarah, her mother, was only nineteen and presumably somewhat irresponsible. After Sarah fled the coop, Florrie and

Maude were brought up by their father, with help from his youngest sister Polly, who lived with them for a while. At first, they attended the village school in Quarndon, and I have a photo of them there, with other village children, after which, my grandmother told me, she had to walk, from the age of ten, all the way to Gerard Street School in Derby, four miles away, passing very few houses until they reached the far side of where Broadway now stands. Florrie and Maude were devoted sisters, very attractive and much alike, usually well dressed in clothes made for them by their father. Pictures of them, now lost, showed them wearing elegant dresses and large Edwardian picture hats. After Polly left to get married (another ill-fated romance, as it happened) the girls took over the housekeeping, and for a while, their grandfather William Shotton seems to have also lived with them, as he appears on the census there in 1911.

Florrie married a coachman, Reginald Hood, in 1908 and they had a daughter, Edna, in 1909. In 1912, a son, Tommy, was born, and in 1913, another daughter. When this daughter was only a week or two old and not yet been christened, Florrie went out to play her violin at a local wedding and got drenched coming home through the fields during a violent storm. She contracted rheumatic fever and died a few days later. The baby was named Florence after her. The following year, her husband was called up and was killed on landing at Gallipoli. The following year, the boy, Tommy, also died, and Thomas Shotton was again left with two small girls to look after. I believe, though cannot confirm, that my grandmother, who had given birth to my mother shortly after baby Florence was born and was now pregnant again, had a breakdown around this time. I don't think she ever really recovered from the loss of her sister, to whom she was devoted. Sometime around then, things start to get confused and very strange.

Around 1917, or so my mother said, the child, Florence, simply disappeared. Mum believed that her grandfather had employed a housekeeper, and this housekeeper had formed a strong attachment to the child and had run off with her. There were rumours that Florence had been taken to America. Or had she been kidnapped for other, more sinister reasons? 'Kidnapped' was always the word that was used. No one seemed to know.

Edna stayed at Vine Cottage and went to the village school. I found her in an old school photograph published in a book and several people remembered her, but no one remembered her having a sister. If my mother was right about the disappearance happening in 1917, then Florence would probably have been too young to go to school. This would make sense. Edna eventually went to live with the rest of the family at the Cavendish along with her grandfather, and she and my mother were very close. She worked at Thurman & Malin's, an exclusive Derby department store (now occupied by McDonald's), after leaving school, and when she was twenty-one, inherited a small legacy from her Great-Grandfather Whieldon (Sarah's father) and went to live in Bournemouth, where she eventually became a fashion buyer for a large department store. After she died, unmarried, in 1961, when my mother and grandmother went to sort out her affairs, they discovered a similar legacy had been left for her lost sister Florence, and had been left untouched in the bank for all those years, hoping that she would one day be found. What happened to it, I don't know.

Almost fifty years later still, an email appeared in my Ancestry.co.uk mailbox relating to a Florence Hood.

The mother or the daughter? I messaged back.

The daughter, came the reply. It was from Florence's grandson. I'd found her at last.

From what we learned from our combined information, the child Florence had been brought up on a farm at Endon Edge, North Staffordshire, not far from where Alton Towers is today, and a surprisingly remote part of the country even now. She had a very happy childhood with a large family called Waterfall, who she always assumed were her blood relations, as did her own daughter, Barbara. It was only after she died in 1982 that Barbara found her mother's marriage certificate stating that her real maiden name was Hood, and she realised to her surprise that her mother was no relation to the family who had brought her up at all. How she came to be with them is still a mystery, though it is possible that a private adoption had been arranged, by either the Shottons or more probably the Whieldons, who did have connections with that area. But why no one else was ever told about this seems very strange.

As there was no official adoption policy in this country until around 1925, children were often farmed out to other families, though usually relatives, if they were orphaned or their parents were having a hard time. And then there was the 'kidnap' story – very odd. Was there really something behind this, or had my grandmother, who seems to have had some kind of breakdown, simply made it up as a kind of bogeyman story when her own children misbehaved? Certainly her own unsettled background must have left her feeling very insecure and she was known to have been 'difficult' at times as a result. It could be that the 'adoption', such as it was, could have been a combination of both possibilities – perhaps a Waterfall daughter had been the Shotton housekeeper, and *had* taken the child unofficially, and then some amicable agreement was reached, since I've always been curious about the lack of investigation that seems to have gone into all this at the time or, indeed, since. But the important thing is that Florence had a happy childhood and was not sent to an orphanage or shipped off to 'the colonies', as they then were, to be used (as, regrettably, many were) as child labour, or abused in any way. And yet, the strangest and saddest bit of the mystery is that her sister, Edna, never knew what had happened to her, and neither did my mother, born the same year, who was always haunted by this story. And indeed, it's just as strange that Florence's inheritance was never claimed.

Edna was Florrie's elder sister, four years older, born in 1909, and she and my mother looked similar and were quite close. After living with Grandpa Shotton, then moving to the Cavendish, she left for Bournemouth and never returned to Derbyshire other than for the occasional holiday, and, after the Second World War, not at all. Neither did she marry, although she did have a boyfriend, referred to courteously by my grandparents as 'Edna's young man'. His name was Charles. Until recently, I never knew his surname and only recognised him from a few photographs as a tall, slim man with curly dark hair and, it would appear, a sense of mystery. No one knew precisely why they didn't marry, but it was implied that Charles was already married and couldn't get a divorce. However, they seemed very happy together, though I am not sure whether they cohabited until later in life when Edna had a stroke, after which Charles seems to have lived with her and nursed her devotedly. Edna was barely fifty when she died. My mother and grandmother went down to help Charles sort out her affairs, which was when they discovered Florrie's unclaimed legacy. This would have been in 1961, shortly after I started work. After this, Charles seemed to disappear off the radar completely. No one knew what had happened to him.

A little investigation a couple of years ago on a family history website eventually gave me his surname and led me to a relative who'd been researching his family. Charles, it appears,

William and Ann Neal(née Dinnis) my gt gt grandparents,c1860 or earlier before William's departure for America and the Civil War.

Charles Neal Snr. Son of William and Ann as a young man. My gt grandfather.

L to R Charles Neal, younger son Vincent Neal, elder son Charles William Dinnis Neal(my grandfather)standing and Lizzie Neal(née Holbrook).

Neal and Morley shop at The Spot, Osmaston Road, Derby, during World War 1. Vincent Neal, who served in the war and was seriously wounded, is on left of picture with shop manager on the right. The shop has changed hands many times but is still there.

Neal family outside their home, the Cavendish, Stenson Road, Derby, c1930. Lto R Gordon, Charles W.D, Maude(nee Shotton, my grandmother), Thomas F. Shotton, her father. The house remains much the same today.

Quarndon Village School. My grandmother (Lilian)Maude Shotton is 2nd R and her older sister Florrie(Florence Ann) 2nd R on the row behind. C1890.

Florrie and Maude as children.

Tom Shotton, sister Polly, Maude and Florrie in the orchard at Vine Cottage, Quarndon.

Shotton home and tailoring business. c1898. Brothers Fred and possibly Gus on L. William and Ann Shotton centre. Lady in hat and the lady L of Ann are either Polly or another sister, Louisa. My grandmother Maude is the girl with the dog and her sister Florence to R of their father, Tom. Both girls look extremely uncomfortable - corsets, possibly? Holding the small girl at far R is Clara, who emigrated to Canada in 1907. The original photo is part of a family archive in museum at Red Deer, Alberta. It was taken in either Barton under Needwood or Walton on Trent. The house, which looks quite substantial, has not been identified. The name Shotton is clearly displayed over the door. William and Ann in smaller premises by 1901.

L to R Tom Shotton as a young man with brothers Bert and Fred.

Outside Vine Cottage, c.1900. L to R Maude, Tom Shotton in pony trap, possibly Thomas Whieldon, Maude's grandfather(father of estranged mother Sarah) and Polly. Thomas Whieldon lived nearby and remained on good terms with the family.

Neal Family Holiday L- R Douglas, Gordon, Marjorie(my mother),Maude, Charles. Dated August 1925 and sent as a postcard to Vincent Neal.

Another holiday. My parents with friends c1931. My father Fred, on right with my mother Marjorie(Madge)next to him.

My mother Marjorie (Madge) Neal

My father Fred on the staircase at The Grove, Duffield Road, Derby, with one of his older brothers behind him, possibly Hodge.

My father Frederick Haddock (Fred).

My parents' wedding, June 1938. Surprisingly, none of their brothers appear on this family group, which shows only the older generation, plus two bridesmaids and Charles Bryant(Dad's cousin)who is best man. His fiancée, Winifred Worth, is the bridesmaid next to him. L to R reads Grandma Neal(Lizzie), Grandpa Shotton(Thomas F.),unknown bridesmaid, my grandmother Mary Ann Haddock(née Hudson), Fred, Madge, my grandmother Maude Neal, auntie Winnie, my grandfather Charles WD Neal and uncle Charlie Bryant.

My paternal grandfather, Joseph Haddock, who died in 1931.

Family at War. L to R Madge in Land Girl uniform,Fred, Douglas Neal in RAF uniform, Maude, in front of our house in Kingsley Road, Allestree early in World War 11.

Family at War. L to R Fred, Madge, Maude, Charles, Douglas(kneeling) in back garden at Kingsley Road.

Allestree Lane c1936,
still only half-developed.

Chester Green.
My father's birthplace.

Chester Green Road, Derby.
The Haddock, Hudson and Bryant
familes all lived here. The Great
Northern Railway ran along the
back of the gardens, where Dad and
Uncle Charlie threw the potatoes
onto passing wagons.

The Grove, Duffield Road, Derby in
2018, under renovation. It's possible
it was not lived in again as a family
home after my grandfather died during
the Depression. Since divided into two
parts, previously offices, now a day
nursery and flats in preparation.

My grandparents former home, Stenson Road, the Cavendish, Derby, photographed c 1995.

First seaside holiday with Mum and Dad. Possibly Bridlington.

With Dad, on holiday.

Another holiday, with Mum, possibly Morthoe.

CORNWALL 1953/1954

My first visit to Cornwall,1953.

Chysaucester,1954.

*The day we got lost
on the moors*

Brenda(2nd L) and best friend Pauline(2nd R) with two younger children and dog Ruffy, Allestree c1951-2.

My first school photo

Quarndon Old Church today. There really is a tower under that ivy.It was largely demolished in 1873. My daughter stands where I used to play with friends. My grandmother's birthplace,Vine Cottage, is lower down the road on the opposite side.

Cromford High Peak Junction, 2019. My granddaughter stands in the old station yard where I loved to go when my father was working there during school holidays. It's now a conservation area.

Site of Bloom Street entry on St Peters St., Derby, where figure is standing, to left of timbered building, which has recently changed hands. It was the former Cheshire Cheese pub and demolition began next to it for the Eagle Centre, now Intu. Our warehouse has gone and Bloom St is just a truncated yard.

The famous ones - Plaque to Herbert Spencer, Exeter Bridge, Derby

The famous ones - Edith Yorke, silent movie actress, signed photograph. Born Derby 1867.

*Brenda with Grandma(Maude Neal)
and Mum(Madge) in back garden at
Stenson Road, with dog Peggy, 1960.*

*Brenda with Gran (Mary Ann Haddock)
Allestree, 1960.*

*The Herbert Strutt Grammar School, Belper,
1959. School Christmas card.*

*On the field at Strutts, L to R -
Holly(Helen), Pauline F., John (a 6th
former who tolerated us), Eileen and
Sandra. 5th form. 1960.*

The former Herbert Strutt Grammar School, Belper, now the Strutts Centre, 2019.

The journey to school. The first green glimpse of the Chevin and Milford tunnel. 2019.

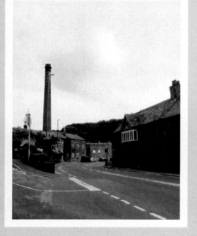

Milford, where the North begins.

The Derwent at Milford.

The Chevin and Babington Hospital.

The Library at Strutts, now being restored. 2019.

The memorial window, Strutts school library.

The alcove where I hid.

SPAIN

STILL SEARCHING FOR MY LOST HISTORY AND 'THAT OTHER WAR'

From my press cuttings collection. Premiere of my first stage play REHEARSAL set in the Spanish Civil War. Derby Playhouse Studio, December 1980. Acknowledgments to Derby Playhouse and the Derby Telegraph.

By Gaudi's menacing hooded figures on a Barcelona rooftop, 2010.

Shadows of that 'other war'. By the trenches near La Fatarella, on the Ebro Front, 2015.

HOME GROUND

The Trent at Burton Bridge.
The river my ancestors followed

My grandchildren exploring the rocks at
Bradgate Park, Leicestershire in 2017.

The ancient rocks of Charnwood, Bradgate Park,
Leicesteshire

Bunkers Hill, Quarndon, where my grandparents used to
picnic and near the site of House that Wasn't There.

Brenda at Bunkers Hill, Quarndon, 2013.

My grandchildren on the Millennium Topograph at Bunkers Hill, 2013.

Brenda Ray, 2019

who outlived Edna by many years ("The most miserable man I ever knew," said the relative, somewhat disparagingly), had been leading something of a double life. Not only did he have a wife, but a remarkable seven children as well, and after poor Edna died – and this is the really incredible bit – he went back to her. Apparently he'd been paying her rent for all those years. How much of this the unfortunate Edna knew, I simply don't know, but I suspect the seven children didn't come into it. Whether Charles had other strings to his bow as well, so to speak, I don't know either. "Did your relative work in a hotel?" asked the lady at the other end of the phone. Er, no. Charles apparently did, though, for I found him on the 1939 Register, made at the onset of World War Two, working in the garage of the Grand Hotel. Of Edna herself, I found no trace.

So what sort of person was Charles, really? To our family, he seemed a decent, caring person and he certainly looked after Edna when her hard times came. I have never heard an ill word about Edna, remembered by everyone as a sweet and gentle sort of girl, a lonely child who had lost all her close family and was haunted by the apparent disappearance of her sister. Who can pass judgement on people from all those years ago who they didn't know and never met? And why, indeed, should they? I hope, wherever Edna and Charles are in the universe now, that they are both happy.

Vine Cottage itself was not finally sold until the late 1930s, not long after my great-grandfather had officially bought it from the Scarsdale Estate when some of Lord Curzon's land was being sold off. Presumably until then it had been rented. I am curious as to why it was actually bought after he had ceased to live in it, but perhaps it had been sublet to someone else. Probably there was some complicated legal reason. By this time he was living at the Cavendish with my grandparents, and my mother said no family member was able to be present at the sale and many valuable items remaining in the house simply 'disappeared'. This again I feel to be slightly odd.

I have various photos of the cottage, taken over the years, including one with Polly and the two girls in the orchard, and another with Tom Shotton, my great-grandfather, in his pony and trap, which also shows Polly and my grandmother, then aged about twelve, and an elderly man I was told was her grandfather, Thomas Whieldon, father of the errant Sarah, though I am uncertain about this. The original central door of the cottage is visible. The horse was called Ben, and had originally belonged to a Captain Jacobson who lived higher up the road, who had sold him to Thomas as a carriage horse after an injury which prevented him from point-to-point racing. There was a lovely but unfinished painting of Ben by a local artist in Grandma's attic, which, along with so many things, 'disappeared' after she died.

Tom Shotton died at the very end of 1939, at Polly's home in Barton-under-Needwood, where he had been sent by the family as a safer place to be in case of air raids, as by this time he was quite infirm. His death was not registered until 1940. Remembered as a kindly man who brought up his two daughters alone, he had a hard life. Despite being London trained, he was a countryman at heart who could dowse for underground water with a hazel twig and could charm wild birds and animals. He seems to have been quite a character and, as with so many of that generation, I wish I could have met him.

THIRTEEN

Edith the Actress

O ne of the other interesting stories that abounded in my grandmother's family was that of a cousin who was an actress and had been a silent movie star in the early days of Hollywood. All I knew about her was her name, Edith Yorke, and that she was a supporting actress who had worked with a lot of big names and was believed to have died from curvature of the spine brought on by constant exposure to the very hot and dangerous studio lights that were used then. No one seemed to know much else about her, except for the title of one film, and the fact that she'd visited the family in Derby a few times and had died in the 1930s. Nobody seemed to know, either, which side of the family she belonged to, though the Shottons, like my great-grandfather Thomas, did have musical and artistic interests. One of Tom's sisters had indeed emigrated in the early 1900s, but to Canada rather than the US.

Having eliminated the Shottons as possibilities, I then had a look at the Whieldons, family of the runaway Sarah, who also, it seemed, had theatrical tendencies, but it was a very long time before I found any connection. The Whieldons were, nonetheless, a faintly mysterious lot, although Grandpa Whieldon had been greatly liked by my grandmother and her sister and had promised to look after them. He had, it turned out, remarried in his old age, a fact I discovered when his will turned up, and it seems that, although he left a legacy to my grandmother (and her absent mother, as already mentioned) and Florrie's daughters as well as his own children, he left even more to Wife Number Two. Whether this went down well with the rest of the family, I don't know. Possibly not. She was probably a very nice person, but second marriages, especially late in life, really mess up one's family research. Wife Number One, who was my grandmother's biological grandmother, had died some twenty years earlier, which I suppose was why my grandmother had never talked about her. It was from her family, apparently, that Edith the Actress had sprung.

The Whieldons, apart from being mysterious, seem to have been a slightly strait-laced, stiff and starchy lot, apart from one charming elderly aunt called Auntie Fanny, and her husband, Uncle Arthur, whom I remember meeting when I was about twelve, the only members of that side of the family I ever met. They were very old then, and lived somewhere in Birmingham. Perhaps having such a renegade daughter as Sarah had caused the rest of the Whieldons such embarrassment that they had simply retreated into their shells, maybe considering that any of her offspring, legitimate or otherwise, were in some way slightly tainted, and they don't seem to have been over-friendly towards our side of the family. My mother only remembered the scary Aunt Eva (real name Evina) who told her off in no uncertain terms when she was seven, causing a fit of umbrage that she still recalled when she was seventy. Eva had a daughter known as Cousin Muriel, whom the family seemed to like, but since going to their house was like walking on eggshells, I think they only went there under sufferance.

Edith the Actress, however, turned out to be related to Whieldon Wife Number One, whose maiden name was Anne Elce, born to a wealthy manufacturer in Manchester, but her ancestors were Derbyshire farming and lead-mining folk called Barker who lived around Wirksworth and Winster. Edith's grandfather had also married twice, which confuses the researcher even more. Mary Ann Barker's mother died when she was only three, and in her teens, she migrated back to Derby from Manchester where she'd been living with her half-siblings and married a railwayman's son called James Murgatroyd who'd come down from Yorkshire. Edith, their first child, was born in Oxford Street, right next to what later became the Derbyshire Royal Infirmary, now the Community Hospital, and next to nothing is left of the street itself except for the nameplate on a wall by the car park. Facing the top of the road is the Royal Crown Derby china factory, which when Edith was born in 1867 was still the parish workhouse. Perhaps this was to influence the early part of Edith's career, and I believe that it did. When Edith was about seven, the family moved to East Hackney, then to Croydon, where James Murgatroyd, who had become a coal merchant, set up business and seems to have done quite well for himself.

Some years later, Edith came back to Derby to work as a schoolmistress in the new Rowditch Workhouse, or Boundary House, later to become the Manor Hospital and opposite the Royal Derby Hospital. Much of the site is now under the Aldi supermarket. Behind it was farmland stretching towards Mackworth in an area called Humbleton, and Edith met and married the farmer's son, Robert Byard, returning to Croydon for their wedding in 1894, before settling in Derby at 183 Parliament Street, near St Luke's Church. Humbleton Farm is now under the Mackworth Estate, and Edith's home in Parliament Street has also gone, although some houses remain. After the death of Edith's father, several more family members came back to Derby, and lived in the same area. Edith had two children while living in Derby, both, according to the records, born in Kilburn, and this *was* Kilburn near Belper, not Kilburn, London, as I double-checked just in case. I couldn't find a record of any family connection there, although nearby Holbrook had a maternity hospital at one time. It looks as though they may have lived briefly in the area between 1895 (when Robert Frank was born) and 1898 (when Freda was born), since Robert's place of residence as the father is given as 'Kilbourn' (old spelling), a sub-district of Horsley. Robert is described as 'master wheelwright'. Robert Byard is later described on the 1901 census as a wheelwright and coachbuilder living at 183 Parliament Street, Derby. Edith is still described as a schoolmistress, but her mother Mary Ann is living with them, presumably looking after the children.

In 1902, Edith and her husband and children emigrate to the United States via Montreal, and settle in Washington State in a place called Wilkeson, in the shadow of Mount Rainier. Later, one of her sisters joins them, and descendants of both families are still living in the area around Seattle to this day. Robert and Edith's relationship seems to be a bit hit-and-miss over the years, with them often living apart. In 1920, a US census finds Edith living in Los Angeles with her daughter Freda, and described as a movie actress. Freda is also described as an actress. Robert seems to be still in Washington State. However, both are present at Freda's wedding to Kenneth Chryst in LA in 1923. The name Chryst was originally spelled 'Christ', though pronounced with a short 'i', but, possibly being a little difficult to live up to, the spelling was changed to Chryst, and the family had originated in Alsace, according to one of their descendants who kindly supplied much of this information.

It seems interesting that both Edith and her daughter are described as actresses, and I have never found any other reference to Freda, unless she worked under a different name, as Edith herself did, though I'm not sure why her name was changed from Byard to Yorke. However, it's rather more Hollywood than Murgatroyd. I can't help wondering if it was Freda who went, as a young hopeful, to hang about outside the studios with her mother as chaperone, but it was Edith who was spotted and got the parts. Movies were a young person's game in those days, and probably the need for older actors was pressing, even untrained ones, as we presume Edith was, since as far as we know she had no experience in acting before this, unless she performed in amateur theatricals during her teaching years.

Edith's son, Robert Frank Byard, became a violinist with a Los Angeles symphony orchestra, after serving with the Canadian Army during the First World War, and Kenneth Chryst, who married Freda, was apparently also a violinist with ambitions originally to be an actor, so that is probably how they all met. Kenneth and Freda went back up north, however, and it is their descendants who are still in the area around Seattle.

Edith herself, as Edith Yorke, stayed in California, working in films from 1919. She made sixty-five films that we know about; the earliest, *The Doctor and the Bricklayer*, in 1919. Charlie Chaplin guest-starred in a film about Hollywood in which she also featured (*Souls for Sale*, 1923), and she also played in a short with his brother Sidney. She played the mother of a young Paul Muni in *The Valiant* in 1929, and was also the mother in *City Girl* (1930), one of F. W. Murnau's three

American-made movies, which I have on DVD. Her biggest role was as a fading actress in *Belle of Broadway* in 1926, a charming little melodrama-cum-comedy which I also have on DVD – and she was *very* good. Grandma was notoriously vague about which films Edith had actually been in, but the only one the family seemed to agree on was something called *Seven Keys to Baldpate*, a thriller made in 1925, and even then they seem to have confused the storyline with that of another film, but Edith was definitely in a film of that name.

The best-known film in which she had a part, though, was the very first, silent, version of *Phantom of the Opera* in 1925, with Lon Chaney. However, a lot of this film is missing, due to deterioration of film stock, and since Edith was in the first part of the film (playing Mamma Valerius, the heroine's adoptive mother), which acts as a sort of prequel to the main story, her section is missing from some abridged versions. I did actually have a video of this, but it seems to have gone missing when I moved house and I've never managed to find it again. Annoyingly, it was one of the abridged versions that was shown in Derby Cathedral recently as part of a film festival, which is a pity, since I'm sure Edith would have been thrilled to know her film had been seen in her home town in the atmospheric setting of our lovely cathedral, which incidentally is almost opposite the site of the Baptist chapel where her parents were married.[3]

Edith's parents must have changed their religious persuasion, since she was christened at the Anglican St Andrew's, that massive Victorian edifice dubbed the Railway Church, on London Road, which was close to where they lived

---

3   By a Reverend Harris Crapwaller, you may be fascinated to know; a
     name which has a certain Salingeresque quality, I think. Being me,
     I simply had to look him up to find out if he was real. He was, and
     I found a whole nest of Crapwallers from whom he was descended,
     somewhere in London. On some records, the name is down as
     Crapweller, but what the heller? Just thought you'd like to know. The
     name still makes me smile.

on Oxford Street, and backed onto Nelson Terrace, where her father had first lived when he came to Derby. Or maybe it was just a matter of convenience. Nelson Terrace is still there at the back of the former sorting office, although no houses are there any more, but since it's so close to the station, many railway people must have lived there. St Andrew's, with its enormous landmark spire, bit the dust around 1970, and St Mary's Gate Baptist Chapel sometime in the 19th century, although the site was for years semi-derelict and later used for parking. Its wrought-iron gates, however, dating from when it was a private residence, now grace the front of Derby Cathedral, so at least some vestige of it remains.

Edith returned to Derby several times and visited the family at the Cavendish, where everyone remembered how nice she was. She may well have had other relatives still living around Derby, too, and also visited her brother who was living in Beckenham, Kent. Her mother, Mary Ann, seems to have gone back to Croydon, where some family members also remained, and she died in 1914.

James Murgatroyd, the brother, visited Edith in the US on several occasions, but we know no more about him, other than that he is recorded as Captain James Oswald Murgatroyd, but whether military, naval or whatever is not noted. His occupation in later life is given as 'coal merchant'. Edith Yorke seems to have last come back to Derby sometime in the early 1930s and made her last (uncredited) appearance in a film called *Luxury Liner* in 1933. She died in 1934 and is buried in South Gate, California. Edith seems to have had a quietly distinguished career as a supporting actress in over sixty films. Not bad for a girl from Derby of quite humble origins.

All in all, it's a shame I don't know more about my grandmother's fascinating family, but there may be things she knew about that she would prefer that others did not. Certainly her mother's disappearance must have affected her greatly, even though she never knew her. When I finally got hold of a photo of the missing Sarah, I must say they did look quite a lot alike, including their taste in hats, and the photograph someone sent me of one of her half-sisters also bears a resemblance. Whether Grandma knew she had seven half-siblings, we will never know, but now at least I know what happened to a couple of them. As for Sarah herself, she was the Picture With its Face Turned to the Wall of Victorian legend. Sarah was, according to the few relatives I've managed to trace, not the easiest of people to live with, as was (not) my grandmother, who was apt to be more than a little temperamental, though considering the traumas of her early life, it isn't entirely surprising. Grandma seemed to have only ever read one book (it was *Rebecca*) and she would usually mention it, but she liked the theatre. When I asked her what play she liked best, she replied, *"Look Back in Anger."*

I was, to put it mildly, gobsmacked. My Tory-voting, hat-wearing, ladylike grandmother? "You mean, Jimmy and Alison and the ironing board, and all that?" I asked.

"That's the one," she replied adamantly. "Best thing I've ever seen. I thought it was terrific!" I can't help wondering what life would have been like if Grandma had married a Jimmy Porter instead of my kindly, ever-patient grandfather! Still, perhaps her own mother found that out during her assorted relationships.

Luckily, my mother's parents seemed to have had a very happy marriage. My grandfather was a quiet, peace-loving man, who loved music. He seems to have been quite adventurous in his youth, however, and was the proud owner of the first motorbike in Derby. Perhaps it was on one of his biking adventures that he met my grandmother, who lived some distance away in Quarndon. He also bought one of Derby's first cars and spent what spare time he had with his children, when work was over, driving around the countryside. Like me, he had a good eye for photography and a good ear for a story. Many of those stories were passed on to his children.

Grandpa's family indeed seemed to have had its share of strange events and mysteries, most especially the American Civil War business. Did the Civil War soldier, William Neal of Wootton, Lincolnshire, really die in the war, or survive and set up a new family and simply not come back? Did he come back as the person with a similar name but differing dates who ended up in Hull Prison a few years later? Or did he never actually go at all? Again, we may never know. But whatever he did, his wife and children seem to have been in dire straits after a few years elapsed. Then the mother disappears off the records too; and the story of the runaway servant seems to have merged with that of one of William's brothers. They were clearly a family that was divided and scattered by poverty and misfortune. One of the brothers, I was shocked to discover only recently, died in Brigg Workhouse in the early 1920s. Did anyone know, or even care?

And what of the wealthy Antills and their slightly less illustrious in-laws, the Holbrooks? And where did the legend that they were related to the Shirley family of Shirley Hall, near Ashbourne, come from? I've never found any connection there at all. But since most of these connections seem to have been through the female line, finding out who married whom is difficult. One of those women stitched the delicate embroidered pictures, two of which I still have, but who was she? Sadly, family history is full of half-remembered facts and Chinese whispers. But at least we really did have an in-law who was a famous philosopher, and an ancestor who was a Hollywood actress.

FOURTEEN

Dad's Family: Clogs to Carriages and Back Again...

Family stories tend to be told by the women, which is perhaps why I know so much more about my mother's family than my father's. If some families are described as 'close-knit' then Dad's might be better described as 'loose-knit', since although they were certainly interesting, with their rapid rise to wealth and back again, they weren't particularly great storytellers. Perhaps Dad's generation being all male had something to do with it, since (apart from my maternal grandfather), as I said, it's usually the women who pass on the family history. They weren't photographers, either; unlike my mother's family, who took loads of pictures but were decidedly careless with them and usually chucked them in an old box or carrier bag somewhere, Dad's family took few but did have one or two professional portraits made. What I have now is an amalgamation of both, with a few of those street or beach photographer's shots printed onto postcards to back them up. Oddly enough, even their wedding photos, of which there is a single full group, shows only the older generation, apart from two bridesmaids and the best man (Dad's cousin, Charlie Bryant), and no brothers on either side of the family. Sadly, I have hardly any photos of the earlier generation of Dad's family prior to this, and only one damaged photo of my father alone.

The Haddocks, Hudsons and Bryants all lived close together in the small terraced houses on Chester Green Road in Derby. Along the back of their gardens ran the old Great Northern or LNER railway line. Dad was the youngest of four brothers and his two boy cousins, the Bryants, lived a couple of doors away. My grandmother (Gran Haddock)'s maiden name had been Mary Ann Hudson, and her sister Ada married Jack (or George) Bryant. I don't really remember him at all. They had two sons, Charlie, who was my dad's age and worked at Rolls-Royce, and Dennis, much younger, the tall, good-looking one, later a tailor by profession, who became a radio operator on a Lancaster at the tender age of nineteen. Aunt Ada was as big and booming as Gran was small, thin and bird-like. They couldn't have been more different. Aunt Ada was always kind, though, and usually kept a handful of sweets in her pocket for any child she met. Most of the men had been railway folk of one kind or another, and the women had worked in mills before they were married, although they never actually talked about this. It seems a pity now that people only a few generations ago tried to hide their working-class roots, whereas nowadays most people are perfectly happy to acknowledge them. They had hard lives. I don't envy the things they had to go through. One thing they didn't seem to have, though, was greed. Greed seemed to be the prerogative of those who had enough already.

Chester Green was, and still is, quite an attractive area, with its large green and beautiful old trees, and of course was close to Derby's Roman site at Little Chester. I wouldn't call it eerie, but it does have a powerful sense of history, once you get away from more recent buildings. Even the church of St Paul seems ancient, although it's actually only Victorian. However, a large factory lay along one side of the Green, and the area would still be defined as working class, but it wasn't poverty-stricken working class. Even so, I don't think Aunt Ada ever had much money – she and Gran had both been born in Derby's old West End, though they never talked about that, either – but Gran's husband Joseph did well for himself. Having begun his working life as an errand boy on the railway, he progressed to clerical work and eventually set up his own business as a bookmaker and graduated from the terraced house on working-class Chester Green to a large Victorian mansion on Duffield Road where they had uniformed servants and several cars. As fortunes and fashions change, the Duffield Road house, called The Grove, was split into two long ago and both parts have recently been up for sale, having been used for years as assorted offices, and now looking very run-down, while Chester Green is heralded as 'highly desirable'. Although it is sad to see the lovely gardens concreted over to be used as car parks, currently weed-strewn and derelict, and the buildings in disrepair, the irony of it would have amused my dad, in a way. Clogs to carriages and back to clogs again in three generations, as he used to say. On my last visit in 2018, the south-facing half of the house was being converted into a day nursery and I was allowed to see inside it for the very first time. Dad would have been pleased. The northern half, which I entered briefly as a child, when it was a dancing school, is still boarded up, awaiting conversion into flats.

One of my dad's earliest memories was of himself and Cousin Charlie Bryant in the Bryants' garden on Chester Green while Uncle Jack Bryant was planting seed potatoes. As he moved along the rows, Dad and Uncle Chas were digging them up again and chucking them onto the wagons of a passing goods train. By the time Dad was in his mid teens, he was living in considerable luxury in a grand house near the area known as Five Lamps, and when he married my mother, she reckoned he'd never eaten anything but steak, chicken, turkey and salmon, but that might have been a slight exaggeration! They had met on the tennis courts at Normanton Rec (now more elegantly known as Normanton Park) next to my grandmother's house at the Cavendish when they were around fourteen, though they didn't marry until well into their twenties.

It looks as though Dad's father, Joseph Haddock, had moved to The Grove sometime well after the 1911 census, since my dad, Fred, had been born that year, and we know he grew up on Chester Green, but by the time he was sixteen in 1925, he was at The Grove on Duffield Road, and in Form IV at what would shortly be renamed Bemrose School. It was then called Derby Municipal Secondary School and I think the site was transferred to Uttoxeter New Road around 1930, where it remains. Dad and his brothers were all very bright at school, but none of them were sent on to higher education, which is a pity, since when their father died, no one had been sufficiently trained to carry on his business. Joseph died very suddenly in 1931 of a heart problem, when my dad was nineteen, and the shock made him ill. Around this time, he began to suffer from acquired deafness. He had already started work on the railway as a clerical worker, although what Dad really wanted to do was teach, and he managed to get a place at teacher training college shortly before the Second World War broke out.

But the War changed everything. Again dogged by illness and (only just) surviving peritonitis, Dad was refused admission to the armed forces. Afterwards, despite working non-stop on the railway for six years and being in the Home Guard, his college place was refused on the premise that places were only available to returning servicemen. This he blamed on the new Labour government of the time and it turned him against them, as it seemed grossly unfair. However, he did teach commercial classes in the evenings to railway trainees, which he enjoyed, but he had always really wanted to work with children. Having been taught myself by one or two 'returning servicemen' (I presume) and, along with a load of other unfortunate children, bullied near senseless, I have to say I think Dad would have done the teaching rather better!

I am curious as to how Dad's father actually became a bookmaker on such a grand scale – after leaving Chester Green, he is recorded as a 'turf accountant' (a posh name for a bookmaker), with a proper office, and is living in some style with servants and a car or two, as his elder sons are now old enough to drive. My feeling is that he may have backed a winner himself and it was a good one. He seems to have been a shrewd businessman. However, he appears to have been a quiet man in many ways, with excellent taste. My mother described him as kind, courteous and a perfect gentleman, although his lifestyle seems to have been quite colourful. At the time he came into money, many large country houses and their contents were being sold off after the ravages of the First World War, and my grandparents went to auctions and bought paintings, silver and furniture. For some, the '20s were good. Little did they know, then, that only a few years later, the Depression would set in, and the whole sad performance would begin all over again.

Grandad and Gran were fond of theatre and especially the music hall, and knew quite a few entertainers, both through the horse-racing business and the theatre itself. One person Grandad knew was Edgar Wallace, the very prolific novelist and playwright, who was also fond of the horses, and was, according to Grandad, a complete mug when it came to losing money, which he did in buckets-full. I do wonder if he may also have known Wallace's half-brother, Marriott Edgar who wrote the Sam and Albert monologues, made popular by Stanley Holloway, although apparently the siblings did not meet until they were in their fifties and both in Hollywood! And while I doubt Grandad knew the Aga Khan, he was definitely acquainted with the infamous Prince Monolulu, the be-plumed racing tipster, whom I remember seeing once on a London station, to my dad's delighted comment – "Good heavens, it's the Prince – I didn't know he was still alive!"

Years later, my husband told me he too had a chance meeting with the Prince, also on a London station, when this eccentric black gentleman in a feathered headdress was accidentally knocked over by some boys, and my husband, who was a student at the time, went to pick him up. "Thank you for helping an old man," he said, and gave him a tip. My husband, who'd never put money on a horse before, took the plunge, and it won.

Dad told me Grandad Haddock had a favourite horse called Priory Park, which he backed repeatedly and it seldom let him down. I recently discovered this horse won the Lincolnshire Handicap in 1927, so presumably wasn't the originator of his good fortune, but all the same, I used the name for the title of a short story I wrote, which is in my story collection *Gondwanaland*, in the hope it might do the same for me. It hasn't, so far, but you never know. The Priory Park of my story can be recognised by anyone local as a thinly disguised

Markeaton Park, and although the story, which involves a post-War murder, is invented, some details are real.

I suppose most people have forgotten now that Derby once had a successful racecourse. I imagine it would have been where Joseph Haddock began his career as a bookmaker, although I do know he and the family travelled all over the country attending race meetings as well. Derby Racecourse was off Nottingham Road, just past where the Pentagon Island is now, and had its own railway station. This wouldn't have been far from Derby St Mary's Goods Yard, where my dad first started work after leaving school, and neither was far from Chester Green, where Dad grew up. Derby Nottingham Road Station was still operational until the mid 1960s, though little used, but the racecourse closed in 1939 on the outbreak of the Second World War, and never reopened. Anti-aircraft guns were positioned on the site, which had once been a Roman settlement. Many interesting remains have been found there. As a racecourse, it was operational for ninety years, and racing had previously been held at two other locations since the 1600s, including Sinfin Moor and The Holmes, an area close to the Derwent, before moving to Nottingham Road in 1848, so Derby did actually have a very long racing history.

Derby Racecourse later became the County Cricket Ground, cold and windy and rather unsuitable for the purpose. My father and his brothers were all cricket fans, as well as ardent Derby County supporters, but none of them liked the County Ground. Many outsiders, especially Americans, are always slightly perplexed that *the* Derby is not run at Derby, and it's a running joke in another story of mine called *Angelina*, in which the narrator goes looking for her long-lost penfriend in the US, that every time she tells anyone she's from Derby, they say, "Where the horse race is?" and she replies wearily, "No, that's somewhere else!" Still, it's no worse than trying to explain why Chatsworth is owned by the Duke of Devonshire and not Derbyshire, or why Nottingham Castle does not look like Chinon or the one in Angers, as per *Robin Hood: Prince of Thieves* and endless other movies. Or indeed, Leeds Castle. In Leeds? Well, no. That's somewhere else.

The grandfather I never knew died in 1931 at the height of the Depression and everything they had was sold off for peanuts. When Gran died in 1960 she had a silver horse-and-jockey racing trophy, one decent painting, her china cabinet (which I still have, though minus most of its contents), and a single fragment of a once-valuable carpet under the coal bucket in her small suburban semi.

The family were fond of opera, and all the sons were music lovers, though only one ever learned to play anything, other than records, presumably. Dad's eldest brother was an excellent pianist, but Dad could only manage a burst of 'Chopsticks'. However, he could memorise and improvise lyrics to just about anything, a talent which I also (alas) inherited, together with the inability to actually play anything. I think what drew my mother, who was a serious musician, to him in the first place, was that he simply made her fall about laughing. Dad's shaving and washing-up repertoire was impressive and ranged from Verdi to George Formby (accompanied on occasions by cheese grater and fork). I honestly don't think I grew up knowing the proper words to anything, but I certainly knew plenty of them. This skill was to come in useful later, as it happened, when I worked for a while in the theatre. Some people have normal parents. I didn't. I'm eternally grateful.

As I've said, Dad's family were not particularly close-knit, being so widely spread in age, and apart from Gran, the only members of Dad's family to whom I was ever close were my cousin Tessa, of whom I've already written, and her father,

Hodge, Dad's elder brother, who lived quite near. His real name was Horace, but only Gran ever called him that. He had an assortment of curious nicknames. To the children he was Uncle Ben. Some people found him difficult, and he could be quite aggressive and was ferociously independent, though I think this was partly due to his unhappy marriage, but his relationship with his children, whom he brought up alone, was good. Hodge always wore an old black beret to conceal his baldness, and rode round Allestree on an ancient bike, spending a great deal of time at the Royal British Legion on Cornhill. He'd served in North Africa and later in Germany as part of the Army of Occupation, where he befriended a German family in Hamburg who were living in dire straits. They remained friends for the rest of his life. He was a real character, a great storyteller, when in the mood; mainly of "During the War..." reminiscences, though sometimes also about the Haddock family's palmier days. He was always very kind to me.

Every Sunday morning, Hodge, Dad and their older brother Jack would meet for a drink at the Markeaton Hotel. I often walked down with them and spent an hour or so at Gran's on Kedleston Road, occasionally pausing en route to pull up a wild horseradish root which grew on the verge in Allestree Lane, if we were having a joint of beef for lunch! I think my parents probably tossed for who should grate the horseradish, as it was a painful, eye-streaming task, but if it was lamb for lunch and it was mint chopping that was required, then that was Dad's prerogative. He always did it with a pinch of sugar on the board. Apart from the ability to cook his own breakfast, mint sauce was his sole culinary skill. Hodge, stubborn as he was, preferred to cook his own lunch, apart from the apple pie which Gran always made for him. I still have a vivid memory of watching her as she chopped up cooking apples to do this, when a long, segmented, worm-like creature emerged and wriggled across the table until Gran dispatched it with a swift whack of her knife! Heaven knows where it came from – I remember her saying they were imported apples, but nowadays anyone would probably sue the supplier. To this day, I always cut up cooking apples with considerable caution.

Incidentally, while trying to find out about the origins of the surname Haddock, which we'd assumed was possibly Welsh, as in Maddock and Craddock and their various spellings, I discovered that it was simply the Anglo-Saxon for 'good luck', and nothing whatever to do with fish. It could also be written as Haddo, Haddow, and Haddon. Pity I didn't know that when I was at school...

Apart from Hodge, Tessa and the Bryants, and an unnamed auntie who was taken to a pub once and asked for a glass of warm water, the only other memorable members of Dad's family seemed to be the Johnsons, who consisted of Uncle George and Auntie Rosie, aka The Rich Ones. Uncle George Johnson was a big, fat, bluff, gruff but genial man, a retired greengrocer, and as research revealed, was not, like the mysterious Deirdre, a blood relative at all, but an in-law. It was actually Auntie, more often referred to simply as Auntie Johnson, who was the relative, a cousin of Gran's, her mother having been the sister of Gran's father. So they were from the Hudson side of the family. Auntie had been born Rosabel Kitchen (there was a family liking for fancy names, evidently), in Lodge Lane, Derby. Mr Kitchen seems to have died when Rosie was quite young and her mother then married a Mr Cotton and they moved to St Helen's Street. Neither of these streets would have been exactly wealthy, in fact quite the opposite, but like Gran, Auntie, it seemed, married well, as they used to say, or at least to someone who knew how to make money. But in Auntie's case, they managed to keep theirs. Their childhoods were probably hard, however, and life was no picnic for any young women born around the West End in the late 19th century. I suspect their early married lives would have been none too prosperous either, but Uncle acquired a greengrocer's shop at 134 Abbey Street, and later, I think, became a wholesaler, and by the time I knew them, Auntie and Uncle were living in well-heeled Horwood Avenue off Burton Road, and were the only people I ever knew who had a maid.

Auntie was thin and querulous with piled-up white hair and hawklike features, reminding me very much of an elderly actress called Patience Collier who was still taking dramatic roles in the 1980s. Sometimes, when I was a child, we used to go on the bus to visit them in their elegant house on Horwood Avenue, which was just a few doors down from the small modernist Swedenborgian Church. A cousin who lived near was a more frequent visitor and said that, as a child, visits were pure hell, with the house only lit by the odd twenty-watt bulb – she used to take a book to read, but it was too dark to see – and freezing cold, but I honestly can't remember that much. With two bus journeys and a walk involved, we probably didn't go that often. I do remember, in later years, taking the dog, at which Auntie would peer suspiciously and enquire, "Is it house-trained?" It was. And so were we.

My main memories are of Sally the maid, Joey the budgie, of whom more later, and Uncle, big and gruff, sitting me on his knee and commenting how some children were a bit scared of him, but I wasn't! I think he quite liked me. My cousin remembered the Johnsons as being distinctly stingy, but Uncle always gave me half a crown, and later his George V crown (five-shilling piece), which I still have, to remember him by.

Dad said in the 1930s, George and Rosie used to drive around in a Rolls-Royce or Rolls Bentley with a churn of ice cream in the back which they doled out to everyone. Uncle died when I was about ten, and Auntie moved to a bungalow over the road. After George died, Auntie got more reclusive and I think it was around this time that she became decidedly on the frugal side, though she was always guaranteed to give everyone in the family a generous wedding gift. Except for me. When it came to my turn, the family member before me, not mentioning any names, had apparently omitted to thank her properly, so I didn't get one. Just my luck.

George and Rosie had one son, also named George Johnson, who was killed in the First World War. I've tried a number of times to find out more about him, but with the name being a fairly common one, it's proved almost impossible. The closest I've found is a George William Johnson who did seem to be their son, born in 1898, but this would have made him very young to have served in the War, although of course many men were. However, he was engaged to be married at the time he died, which again is surprising, since he would only have been twenty by 1918. Of course, I don't know in what year he died – he could have been one of the unlucky ones who so nearly made it to the end. I am certain he died in action, not in the influenza pandemic after the war, but that's all I know.

The girl he was engaged to was a Miss Mary Eno. She was one of three sisters, all army nurses, all of whom lost their menfolk in that same conflict. Only the eldest had married. The next sister in line was Miss Mabs, and she and Miss Mary lived in Balderton near Newark in Nottinghamshire. I met all three of them once when they visited Gran at Kedleston Road, all sandy-haired, freckled and cheerful, the last of that generation of indomitable spinsters and widows who dedicated their lives to serving others.

The Miss Enos, who sometimes got called the Miss Epsoms, and possibly also the Andrews Sisters, as one of them told me, would sometimes come to visit Auntie and very occasionally (and unwisely) take her out for a trip in their car. This was always accompanied by Sally the maid, and Joey the budgie in his cage. ("I am not taking that bliddy bird in its bliddy cage in my car ever again!" Miss Mary, or possibly Mabs, announced in her exasperated, clipped English one final time, much to our delight.) Once, years later, when my parents had a car again, they visited the Miss Enos' address in Balderton to find someone else living there and concluded sadly that they must have died. Like George Johnson Junior, whom I never knew, and who to me was just a good-looking young man in uniform in a photograph on Auntie's sideboard, they were part of a generation that had gone forever.

Auntie outlived most of her own generation by a long chalk, and by the time she died, unfortunately, most of the younger ones had given up on her, since visiting had become more and more of an ordeal. I think she left her bungalow to Sally and probably the rest of her wealth to George's nephew (another George, taken perhaps as a substitute for her long-lost son) and his wife, who I believe must have been the parents of the aforementioned Deirdre; probably the only ones to stay the course, so to speak. They lived in Burton, at the only time I remember meeting them, in a house which was demolished shortly afterwards to make way for the A38 Burton bypass. I never did meet Deirdre again. But I remember her picture on a sideboard, too.

FIFTEEN

More Fleeting Memories of Slightly Odd Relatives: Embarrassments in Grimsby and Burton

W hile most of Dad's relatives seemed to remain in the Derby or Burton area, some of Mum's still lived in Lincolnshire, although I have never managed to visit the village where they actually originated, a place called Wootton, not far from what is now known as Brigg. On older records, it was called Glanford Brigg, and other villages where family members lived were Winteringham and Keelby. Lincolnshire is a big county, and they seem to have moved around a lot, mainly in search of employment, although usually returning ultimately to the place of their birth. However, some of my great-grandfather's siblings moved to

Grimsby and I do have a vague preschool-age memory of going there, a visit which had unfortunate consequences. Grimsby itself, and it's not a name which inspires confidence, seems to linger in my mind as a place – then, anyway – of tall Victorian houses with avenues of rather gloomy trees, and the one thing I remember which still exists, a tall, strange-looking tower shaped like a needle near the docks. We stayed with an aunt and uncle called Mabel and Bill, and it was Mabel, I think, who was the relative, a daughter of my great-grandfather's sister, Maria. They had no children, as I recall, which is probably why Uncle Bill was so careless as to leave a razor lying around, probably on the edge of the bath or somewhere, where a small and evidently very stupid (or just curious) child like me would pick it up and try to shave with it like Dad did. Needless to say, I managed to slash my face all over and presumably emerged dripping with blood. I can't actually remember the incident myself, only from hearsay, but I was probably screaming like a banshee as well. As, indeed, was everyone else, when they saw me.

According to my mother's brother, one of these Grimsby cousins was married to a ship's carpenter, who had apparently sliced off his finger during the course of his work, and kept it pickled in a bottle with the proviso that it should be buried with him when he died. I don't think this was Bill, but perhaps accidentally slicing things up or off was a family trait. Another of the Grimsby family members had a parrot which apparently bit a lump out of his lip during a moody moment, but I can't remember who. I seem to remember being told there were three sisters, Mabel, Edith and Annie. I never met Annie, though I may have met Edith, who was married to Percy. Now, Percy sounds like the sort of guy who'd have a parrot, especially if he was a ship's carpenter. People connected with ships tend to have parrots. And that's all I can remember about

Grimsby. Since it had a rather unsettling feel to it, I used the tall, dark houses and needle-shaped tower in a near-future dystopian story I wrote, which I haven't yet published. It seemed somehow appropriate.

The other childhood incident in which I tried to cut off a portion of my face occurred in Burton-on-Trent – Henhurst Hill, to be precise. Or "En'urst 'Ill', as my dad's colleague, whose house we were visiting at the time, preferred to call it. So with him being only a work colleague, this was not a family occasion, but embarrassing, just the same. They too were a childless couple, and his wife, who was rather posher than Jacko, and didn't say "En'urst 'Ill', offered me a drink in a glass, saying, despite my mother's protestations, "Oh, she'll be fine." But of course, being only two or three or whatever and only used to drinking vessels made of chewable plastic, I promptly bit a chunk out of it. I didn't draw blood on this occasion, but was formally presented with the glass, which was a rather pretty frosted one with a bite-shaped piece taken out of it, which its owner possibly thought I'd like as a souvenir. It glowered at me for some time on a shelf in the kitchen until my mother finally decided to bin it. I shall never pass a sign to Henhurst Hill without remembering this slight misdemeanour. Pity, really, as Henhurst Hill was the one place in Burton I remembered as a child where it wasn't permanently raining and didn't smell violently of hops.

Burton in the 1950s seemed to live under a perpetual cloud of drizzle and strange-smelling steam, and was possibly the most dismal dump on the face of the earth. I remember getting off a train there once to meet up with Dad and the man at the ticket gate saying morosely, "Can't think what anyone would want to come here for," which left Mum and me hastening out into the drizzle, giggling.

Now much cleaned up, the Burton of today is a place of not inconsiderable charm, provided the wind is in the right direction, and surprisingly photogenic. I often go and walk by the river and take pictures of the same stand of trees beside the Trent, looking deceptively placid here. I like the marketplace and St Modwen's Church, the gold-mine charity shops, and some of the fine examples of truly eccentric architecture. There's an eerily Gothic cemetery at Stapenhill, which also boasts those two white-stuccoed buildings which appear to have been dropped directly from New Orleans, one of which is the infamous haunted Post Office, once occupied by the Shotton family to whom we were *not* related, and the other is, of course, the old police station which seems to have strayed there from New Delhi. It rarely rains, except on the day when I went to try and sell some books, when, of course, it threw it down so hard you couldn't see across the road. It's a town which has massively improved, while still hanging on to plenty of its old and crummy bits, and I respect that. And it's the only place where I have ever seen a woman try on a sequinned evening gown over the top of a tracksuit. Without the benefit of a changing cubicle.

Also living in the Burton area was the oldest person I ever knew, my grandmother's aunt, known to the family as Auntie Polly. She was my great-grandfather's youngest sister, and at one time, before her marriage, had lived with him in Quarndon, helping him bring up his two daughters. Her maiden name was Mary Miles Stevens Shotton and she was barely thirteen years older than my grandmother, Maude Shotton. However, when she married in 1895, she went to live in Tutbury, that small, fascinating place in East Staffordshire, with its ruined castle on a hill, that's too big for a village and yet not quite big enough to qualify as a town, although apparently it once did. John of Gaunt had lived there, with his second wife, Constantia of Castile, and at one time, the place was known as the Kingdom of Castile, and once a year, for many centuries, a bull was chased through the streets in her honour. Perhaps that's one of the possible sources of a Spanish connection in my family – who knows? Perhaps descendants of Constantia's household are there even now. At least one ancestor on the other side of my mother's family was born there, too.

And then, of course, there's Dad's family, who seem to have originated from Kings Bromley, another Staffordshire village not far away, with their dark hair and eyes, straight features and passion for football, music and horses – what could be more Spanish than that? DNA testing seems to indicate that any Spanish/Iberian genes in my make-up amount to only about 5%, with another 5% from Southern Europe generally. Whether or not this counts the Basques as well (whom I've believed for a long time may have settled in Iron Age Derbyshire and Staffordshire, where their distinctive features can be seen among farming and former lead-mining communities to this day), I cannot say. And nobody really knows where the Basques and their unique and unconnected language actually originated. We humans, and our distant ancestors, are curious creatures, after all.

But to return to my oldest remembered relative, Polly lived in Monk Street (one of the smaller streets lower down from the castle, near where, years later, I was to take my infamous and unexplained ghost photograph) with her charming but useless husband, Arthur King. Arthur was a stonemason from Buckinghamshire who had been working on one of the local churches when they met. Marriage to Arthur seems to have been a bit of a disaster. I'm not sure when he stopped working as a stonemason, but it appears that before long it was Polly, not Arthur, who was both property owner and breadwinner. A few years after their marriage, they ran a farm-cum-pub together; the Blue Bell at Anslow. In those days, some village pubs only had a two-day licence to sell liquor, usually on market days, and this seems to be the case with the Blue Bell, where they were living in 1907. The rest of the time, it was a working farm, belonging to Polly, who we believe had inherited it from an elderly neighbour to whom she had been kind, although again, stories vary as to which of the properties she owned this actually was. Polly seems to have had a number of different homes after leaving Barton-under-Needwood where she was born in 1873, and at one stage she was believed to have been quite a wealthy woman. However, she was not as lucky as she sounds.

Various stories abound about Polly's marriage and the feckless Arthur – marrying feckless charmers seems to have been a Shotton family trait – but the oft-quoted version is that Arthur departed early one morning around 1910 while she was still asleep, taking a herd of their cattle which he sold at market, bought a one-way ticket to Canada and went off prospecting for gold. And that, as far as we know, was the last she ever saw of him. I do now know, via a distant relative out there, that he did indeed settle in Canada, in Alberta, and made a land grant application around ten years later, quoting for a 'wife' he claimed had lived with him for some time, and we know was not Polly! However, according to Canadian records, the township in which he settled failed and was abandoned. Presumably he moved on, since he made other applications, and at one stage, still quoting for a wife, seemed to be classed as a farmer. Eventually, we lose track of him, although there is a record of someone we think may have been him dying in Hanna, Alberta in 1938.

Polly, by now living and farming back in Barton-under-Needwood, made a will in 1939, still describing herself as 'married', though she lived on until 1965, when I last saw her in the Andressey Hospital in Burton, shortly before my twenty-first birthday. Several of Polly's dates in the official records seem to be a bit vague, and her date of death is certainly wrong, as both I and another family member can qualify. Polly had a long life, most of it spent as a lone woman farmer in various parts of Staffordshire, but her last two homes were in Barton-under-Needwood. I didn't see her often, as we didn't have a car until I was nineteen or twenty, so any visits were made with other relatives and very occasional, but her final home was a smallholding down a rutted track outside the village, with the massive cooling towers of Drakelow Power Station looming in the distance across the fields. After she died, it was discovered that Polly owned several other properties in the area as well as land, and the profit from letting them had been milked off for years by a bent solicitor. I believe he was eventually debarred, or whatever they do with bent solicitors, though personally I'd stick them in the stocks, since Polly died in relative poverty.

Grandma said Polly had been a smart, elegant woman in her youth, with lovely auburn hair, who was greatly admired. I remember her as a tall, proud old lady who loved the land and her animals. She had a hard life, in many ways, but remained independent and undaunted, a truly liberated woman. I wish I'd had the chance to know her better.

One of Polly and my great-grandfather's sisters was called Clara, and she was also born in Staffordshire, but further south into the Black Country, in 1866, before the family moved back to Barton and Walton. Clara also had beautiful auburn hair, and became a student teacher. A length of her hair was said to have been woven into a tapestry in Lichfield Cathedral as the hair of an angel, or so my grandmother told us. This always sounded like a piece of family legend worth investigating, though I never managed to do so. However, another family member whom I found some fifteen years ago during family research was equally intrigued and wrote to the cathedral historian to ask about it. Much to our surprise, he was rewarded with a photo of said tapestry, which turned out to be an altar cloth rather than the wall hanging we'd imagined, and showed several angels with cap-like hairstyles which were revealed, as much to the historian's surprise as ours, to be made of human hair! It was not the flowing Pre-Raphaelite style that I'd envisaged, but still rather remarkable and most unusual. Some had been repaired with embroidery thread, the lady said, but most of the angels were definitely blessed with red-gold human hair, and the altar cloth was very special and sometimes brought out at Easter and on other important occasions, though when I visited in 2019, it was in store and inaccessible. Still, another piece of family legend was proved to be true, and Clara's lovely hair lives on in Lichfield, even though its owner died many years ago on the other side of the Atlantic.

Clara married a man named Jack Sleath from Streethay, who seems to have been an army man. Like the Shottons, his family apparently originated from the area around Newport in Shropshire. They had two small daughters, Kathleen and Maude, and in 1907 emigrated to Canada, Jack sending my great-grandfather a long and detailed letter about their journey a year after they settled in Red Deer, Alberta. The reasons for their departure seem to have been complex, and he mentions *more than our share of rough usage meted out to us in the Old Country from one and another*, which sounded odd, and, together with a further comment, made me wonder whether their problems might have been political in origin or due to some kind of family dispute, but a descendant I met some years ago told me the references may simply have related to the loss of another child. Or was it to do with a business? Jack seems to have had several businesses after leaving the army. Perhaps they did not thrive. *There seemed to be nothing left for us to do but try our luck in another land*, he wrote. Yet another reason may have been that Clara was suffering from tuberculosis, and I was sad to learn that she had died after barely two years in Canada, their hope of a cure in a better climate coming to nothing.

Jack Sleath's brother, also an army man, served in India, and married an Indian lady in Calcutta, where my husband's family were to end up, though they did not originate there. So I was not the only Shotton-connected person to have married into an Indian family! However, he seems to have died after only a few years, and his wife appears to have remarried, which makes me suspect she may have been an Anglo-Indian, as she had a Welsh-sounding name (Gwyndon Ophelia Matthias), although on the wedding photograph someone sent me, she looks fully Indian; dark-skinned and very good-looking. A Hindu or Muslim woman would have been less likely to remarry. Perhaps she was a Catholic convert from the South. She was certainly attractive. They don't seem to have had any children together. However, I now know that she did have children from a happy second marriage, whose descendants are living today.

Correspondence with this side of the family continued until sometime during World War Two, as far as I can work out, when the connection was broken. But the long letter from Jack Sleath to my grandfather Thomas Shotton was saved, and after considerable pre-Internet searching, I managed to re-establish some contact with a few of the Sleaths' descendants and eventually with Louise Perkins, whose grandmother was Jack's sister. Louise has done a massive amount of research into both families, so we were able to pool our resources, now greatly aided by Internet websites as well, and have met a couple of times. She still lives in Alberta. She also furnished me with what little we know about Polly's husband, the straying Arthur King, but we don't believe there was any connection between him and the Sleath or Perkins families. Probably they had all washed their hands of him completely. While they, apart from the tragic Clara, seem to have done okay for themselves, it doesn't look as though Arthur ever found his pot of gold.

SIXTEEN

Missing Places

Over the years, Derby and its surrounding areas have lost an awful lot of places. Bill Bryson, in one of his books, comments about Britain being horrendously careless with its history. He'd have a field day with Derby. Derby is a town with a long history, it's produced plenty of talent, a wealth of engineering, rather more famous people than anyone cares to mention (and usually they don't), and is a sort of architectural war zone. Which is ironic, since during the Second World War, it only suffered two serious air raids, despite being a prime target because of Rolls-Royce, and also for being the hub of the railway system. Just outside Derby Midland Station was a massive reinforced-concrete blockhouse known to railway folk as The Kremlin, which housed the communications system for the whole of the Midland Railway. It took them years to demolish, once the War was over. Derby Station itself, of course, as already mentioned, suffered air raids in both World Wars.

One of the reasons why Derby survived the war fairly intact was due to the mist from the River Derwent, which apparently even today makes it quite difficult to spot from the air, and this cloak of invisibility was aided by a collection of smokescreens (bins that burned foul black oil), much hated by locals but efficient at the job. Buildings were also camouflaged, mainly by the designs of a local artist, Ernest Townsend, a brilliant painter and one of Derby's relatively unsung heroes. There was a decoy factory, known as a starfish site, near Aston-on-Trent, which distracted enemy planes, some of which later dropped their loads on or near the Nottinghamshire village of Cropwell Butler, on much the same bearing, the inhabitants of which must have been none too delighted. Rolls-Royce was bombed just the once, in the early morning of the 27th July 1942. My mother witnessed the plane, as she was on her way to work at the market garden, as it swooped over the bus on which she was travelling.

According to various eyewitnesses, it has become clear that there was more than one German plane circling around Derby that morning (experts claim there usually were), but only one dropped any bombs. It was still one too many and twenty-three people were killed. There were, of course, other miscellaneous attacks, most of which killed a few innocent civilians, one being on Jackson Avenue, close to what was then the City Hospital. I've often wondered whether that was the intended target, having been mistaken for a factory. One poor woman died of her injuries. Others are now recorded on the War Memorial. Mercifully, we were spared the horrors of what happened in Coventry and Birmingham. My mother recalled seeing the hideous glow in the sky on the night of the great raid on Coventry. Dad told me returning bombers often dropped their unused payloads over the hills and moors in the Peak District when he was working up at Longcliffe and such places on the High Peak Railway, where he saw the hills burning. I'd like to think they dropped the stuff where they thought it would do less harm, but it was probably only because the crews daren't return to base with a full bomb bay.

Having survived relatively unscathed, shortly after the War, rather than being satisfied with merely implementing the Central Improvement Scheme and finishing off the Council House, a project begun just before its onset, the then-town council began busily demolishing everything else of architectural interest as well, including the wonderful timbered house in Tenant Street known as The Mayor's Parlour, reputed to be one of the finest half-timbered structures in Northern England, simply because some civic person didn't like seeing it from his office window. For years the gap it left was simply used as a bus park. By the time I'd left school and was starting work, I had just become interested in old buildings and their history, and they were vanishing like melting ice. Most of the attractive department stores, some of which had been purpose-built and some adapted Georgian town houses, bit the dust, along with our only Georgian square, St Alkmund's Churchyard and ancient Bridgegate. St Alkmund's Church itself, with its massive Victorian spire, was perhaps no great architectural loss, having been damaged in a gale, but the Georgian square surrounding it certainly was. The only advantage of this was that the Pugin-designed St Mary's Roman Catholic Church was now visible once more, the Anglican St Alkmund's having been, allegedly, built taller in order to hide it, in what can only be described as a truly un-Christian gesture. Then, of course, the dreaded Inner Ring Road carved a swathe out of the middle of town, so that the poor church is now entered by a footbridge over a motorway. If ever a town had its own self-destruct mechanism, Derby is that town.

One strange memory that I have – or was it just a dream? – is of coming into town quite early one pale, frosty, very cold morning around the time I had just started work, and finding that almost everything seemed different. All that had been familiar had gone. The streets were greyish-white and lifeless with an eerie glitter, and half the buildings between Five Lamps and the cathedral simply weren't there any more. Great chunks of our history had been ripped away. The cathedral, thank God, is still there, visible for many miles across the Derwent Valley. Only Boston Stump is taller.

The countryside was changing, too. Another of my strange memories – or was it just another dream? – involves a house that wasn't there. Possibly it was never there at all. One day, I remember being in a family member's car – it must have been my grandfather's, since my parents didn't have one at this stage. I would have been nine or ten. We were driving along the A6 past Burley Hill, just after the last entrance to Allestree Park and the bottom of Burley Lane, when across the fields as we approached the area known as Flaxholme, I noticed a large white house, several fields back from the road. "What's that big white house?" I asked my mother, who was next to me. Why did I ask? Why did it seem special? Why had I never noticed it before?

"It's just a shell," she replied. "It burned down before the War." No more was said.

I did not know it then, but in a few years' time, I would pass that way every day for six years on my way to school and always look for it. I never saw it again. The house was, as I remember it, a long, two-storey white-stuccoed house, quite symmetrical, with either a flat or low-pitched roof and possibly two or three windows on either side of a front door. It looked Georgian or Regency and was quite conspicuous, catching the light, although why I should have asked about it,

I don't really know. I've checked many times to see if I could find any details of a large ruined house in the vicinity. The only contender would be Farnah Hall, just outside Duffield; abandoned, not burned, in the 1920s (though records of the date vary), but it was on the B5023 Wirksworth Road, rather than the A6. Could I have mistaken the route? But no, I'm sure I didn't. Farnah would not be so distant across the fields, and fragments of ruins can just be glimpsed among dense scrub, but there is a gatehouse still, beside the road itself, whereas 'my' house was set further back with no noticeable drive or lodge and the aspect was quite open. Farnah's ruins are apparently part of a former stable block rather than the hall itself, which had been more or less finished off by the Home Guard during the Second World War, who used it for target practice. When I finally came across a couple of photographs of Farnah Hall as it used to be, it was neither stuccoed nor symmetrical, so it's unlikely to have been Farnah or its ghost that I saw. Do buildings themselves have ghosts? I'm inclined to suspect that they do.

My cousin and her farmer husband eventually came to farm at Burley Grange, a large, rambling farmhouse halfway up Burley Hill, and even when we visited them, although this was many years later, I never thought to ask about the white house. Not far from them, higher up Burley Lane, stands a large, beautiful, white modernist house which I had thought could have been mistaken for my mystery building. But it is largely hidden behind a high fence, too far back from the road. The last time I went up there, I was saddened to see it empty and the garden sold off for development. I hope the house, at least, survives. Unforgivably, another attractive modernist house beside the A6 had its flat roof pitched and is now languishing in a terrible state of repair. Is nothing sacred? Burley Grange itself, ancient as it was, bit the dust after my cousins retired and moved away, to be replaced by a huge and incongruous modern structure. But Bunkers Hill, strange and mysterious, with its little twisted trees and massive panorama, where long ago I heard the hummadruz on a summer's afternoon, still remains. Of the mysterious white house, there is no sign at all, but I still look for it every time I go past. And it did generate one of my weirder short stories...[4]

Quarndon itself has many eerie parts, especially around The Common, where there are many large old houses, some with extensive grounds, down long, dark drives, a number of which, according to my grandmother, were reputed to be haunted. One, closer to the new church, even had a family vault in the garden. All fodder for the childish imagination.

I have a memory, too, of another white, flat-roofed modernist house, somewhere, that I seem to have visited. It had metal-framed windows and a distinctive smell, as though it had been closed up for some time. Where was it? Who did it belong to? I have no idea. There are two houses like this by the A6 in Darley Abbey. Could it have been one of those? Certainly it was not the wonderful curvilinear house called Park Gates opposite Darley Park, nor the one previously mentioned on Burley Lane. The one I remember was plainer and box-like, yet elegant. I can still see that house in my mind's eye and smell its curious smell. Perhaps I knew it in another life. White houses seem to haunt me. And they supply me with stories.

Sometimes my dad would be asked to work at Cromford, on the High Peak Railway, and I would go up there with him during the school holidays, occasionally with Mum as well, and I would play in the yard, which smelled of train smoke, oil and sawdust, and walk along the steep path beside the incline where the wagons of limestone were hauled on cables. The part we often walked along was engagingly called Sheep Pasture

---

4   In The Hermit Crab. Gondwanaland, 2013.

Incline. I once saw a baby grass snake wriggling between the lines up there, and Dad remembered seeing one of its larger relatives whipping across the surface of the canal in elegant loops. There were several inclines, apparently, and higher up one reached the equally engagingly named Hopton Top. The Internet now devotes several pages to the High Peak Railway and Cromford Canal. I never realised then that one of my childhood playgrounds was so historically important.

A wharf lay alongside the Cromford Canal adjoining High Peak Junction and it was fun walking along the towpath, through the echoing dark tunnel with dripping walls and then out again, back to the wild plants and the sharp, clean smell of limestone. It was one of my parents' favourite places, and when Dad worked there, during their lunch breaks, they used to play cricket in the station yard. There were only a few mineral trains along the line, though, even then, and I never remember much traffic on the canal. Eventually, a sewage works was built over the far side of the canal, which rather spoiled its charm, and sadly, as a recent visit showed, it is still there, pungent as ever. However, the High Peak Railway is now a walking trail and the Derwent Valley Mills are classed as a World Heritage Site, and the canal is restored but the trains are gone and many of the mills are just museums now. I'm glad I saw them in their latter days, when they were still working.

SEVENTEEN

Moving On

Not long before I took my scholarship exam (aka the Eleven Plus), my parents decided to move house. It wasn't really a bold move – just over the road, in fact, to a two-bedroom bungalow next door to our friends. This would have been early in 1955, so I would still have been ten rather than eleven. I can't remember much about the exam itself. I don't remember feeling particularly nervous. Exams never did bother me much. Strangely, I can't remember an awful lot about our original house, either, except for the garden, the irises and the front room, which was the nicest room, the one we didn't use much. Why not, I wonder? Perhaps because houses were difficult to heat in those days, with only coal fires and, if you were lucky, a small electric one. Or was it because so much of it was taken up by the baby grand piano? Everyone then, before the advent of the through lounge, seemed to have a 'best room', and this was ours, reserved for when visitors came. One thing, perversely, which I do remember, was that there was a small hole in the white hearthrug, burned by a stray spark, which the dog was trained to lie over when anyone came. This he did, with hardly the need to be asked, as soon as anyone who wasn't one of us entered the room, scooting across the carpet to the assigned spot without so much as a conspiratorial grin. In terms of sheer intelligence, not to mention a sense of humour, he and the jackdaw were the two most intelligent creatures I'd ever met.

The back room seemed to be where we sat in the evening. No TV then, so we listened to the radio or played some kind of card or board game, or just chatted. My parents listened to music more than anything, I suppose, and occasionally radio plays and comedy programmes. Because of my dad's hearing problems, it was hard for him to concentrate on programmes that didn't have a specific storyline, so while Mum and I loved *The Goons*, Dad couldn't follow them at all! My parents wouldn't have a TV until I had got through my O Levels, which I suppose was a wise move, though I did watch neighbours' sets occasionally, mainly our Scottish neighbour's, after we'd moved. TV was very limited in the early 1950s, of course, with only one BBC channel to contend with, and only broadcasting for a few hours every evening. Midlands ITV didn't appear until about 1956, when I was eleven. Anyone who had that was really trendy.

Dad actually enjoyed surreal humour and loved the short plays of N. F. Simpson that were shown in the mid '60s, as he said so many things he heard sounded like Simpson dialogue to him anyway! It was just that he needed a visual image to prop it up. I can't remember what he thought of the Pythons – perhaps they didn't emerge until after he died – but he would have loved *Father Ted*. Northern comedy was preferred. Al Read, Ted Ray and assorted Liverpool comics etc. were okay. Max Miller was considered deeply vulgar.

Maybe there is a North-South divide regarding this. I'm not sure where the line is. Possibly south of Birmingham. However, there always seems to have been a lack of Midlands comics. Okay, I know, Jasper Carrott, but he came later. And as someone has reminded me, Tony Hancock, with whom I share a birthday. Sid Field... okay, sorry, Birmingham! But East Midlands? Where are you? Strange, actually, since East Midlands folk in particular tend to be pretty witty. My dad was a very funny man. When someone once asked me, when I'd been writing comedy stuff for a while, who my influences were, I had to say, "My dad, Ken Dodd and Ronnie Barker." Dad adored *The Two Ronnies*, but Ken Dodd, because of his speed of delivery, he couldn't follow.

The back room in our old house, always called the dining room, had French doors that opened onto the garden. The patio door hadn't been invented yet and neither had the patio. When we first heard the term, we thought it was hilarious. Pretentiousness was not something my family appreciated. You had a yard, and you had a garden. That was it. The kitchen of our old house was small but had a black-and-white tiled floor which at least looked nice when it was washed. The bungalow, on the other hand, had that speckled flooring that tends to look like freeze-dried vomit, and was a source of great discontent to my mother, who never felt it looked clean. On the other hand, the kitchen was much larger, lighter, and had room for two large tables. It also had ants. The ants were a joyless discovery, made when coming home from our first holiday after moving in, and finding them swarming up the walls. Our friends next door also had ants, but theirs seemed to be a different, smaller, species. We tried introducing them in the hopes they might annihilate one another, but presumably they simply interbred.

In many ways, I regretted the move, since I liked the semi-detached house better, as the bedrooms, being upstairs, seemed so much more private, and I liked the garden, too. However, there was the incident of The Little Brown Man still playing on my mind, and it meant we were no longer sharing an adjoining wall and garden with our more-than-a-little-deranged neighbours. Apart from them, I was never entirely sure why my parents decided to make that move, as it meant considerably downsizing (another term that hadn't been invented in 1955) and selling the baby grand piano, among other things. Perhaps they were already thinking about retirement, but that seemed a long way off. However, my mother managed to exchange the baby grand for a very good upright, which, alas, I never learned to play, despite her efforts. Eventually, she acknowledged that I was frankly useless, and didn't push it. My talents, as I put it, lay elsewhere. Quite why my grandmother never offered her back her original upright piano, which was still languishing unplayed in her middle room, I simply don't know, since the piano belonged to Mum. The baby grand had been a wedding gift from my father's family and had originally been in their big house on Duffield Road. Mum's own piano continued to languish in Grandma's middle room until after she died and it was commandeered by another relative, without her say-so, who couldn't play it either. However, I'm sure Mum would be pleased to know her second upright piano, which I sadly never mastered, now lives in London, where it is played by my son-in-law, and very well, too. Hopefully, my grandson will master the art, but I never build my hopes too far...

One of the things I didn't miss about the old house, apart from The Little Brown Man and the mysterious whirring thing in the porch, was the gap by the banisters. This was an extremely narrow space, down which anything you dropped tended to disappear. It was fatal to drape anything over the upstairs banister, since if it slid off, it would vanish into a bottomless pit which lay between the stairs and the hallway below. Presumably it wasn't completely bottomless, as some things could, in fact, be rescued, possibly because they had caught on something, and my dad had a special gadget, known as the Haddock Hooker, a billiard cue with a bent pin on the end, which he had designed for this purpose. He claimed that when we left, he offered this piece of essential equipment to the very superior lady who moved in, but it was turned down with a politely supercilious "No thank you." Doubtless she lost a lot of knickers that way.

Although the bungalow was next door to the one I considered to be haunted, where I'd seen The Pin Man, I never had any bad feelings in our new home. It felt a bit strange to begin with, as new or unfamiliar houses usually do, but I soon got used to it. In fact, on looking back, there was slightly more creepiness about our old house, but maybe that's just because I was young and imaginative and couldn't remember it so well. At the back of the bungalow was a structure always referred to as the sun lounge, since it wasn't substantial enough to be classified as a conservatory, and had huge picture windows and a flat glass roof. It was great for in-between seasons, but freezing in winter and far too hot in summer. A paraffin stove was acquired for use when it got too cold, but I hated the smell, as well as carrying the stuff from the shop, which usually fell to me. Eventually, my parents had the living room extended and the sun lounge became part of it, which was a much better arrangement. We didn't have a separate dining room, though, which I always missed.

Many meals were eaten, and homework done, on one of the kitchen tables. In the evening, we tended to eat in the lounge. Even so, although it was a nice house, I always felt a certain lack of privacy there. It was into the garden of the bungalow that I ran, one day after school, to tell my mother, who was talking to our Scottish neighbour, Mr Brown, that I'd passed the Eleven Plus, and would be going to the Herbert Strutt Grammar School in Belper. A whole new chapter of my life was about to begin.

EIGHTEEN

Where the Derwent Flows
By the Chevin

Where the Derwent flows by the Chevin
On its far way to the sea
There's a school beside the high road
That belongs to you and me...
(Strutts School song)

I can't actually remember that first day at school. All I can remember about the early days there was how enormous it seemed, after our small collection of whitewashed prefabs. And how easily, to begin with, you could get lost.

There were two school buses. On the way there, the girls went upstairs on the first double-decker to arrive, and the boys downstairs. Presumably this was so a member of staff or a conductor could keep an eye on them. Girls, obviously, could be better trusted. On the way home, there was a girls' bus and a boys' bus. Perhaps this makes sense to somebody. Our two buses went along Allestree Lane and Kedleston Road, while another went from Derby to Belper and back via Darley Abbey and Duffield Road. We had the privilege of a bus pass. If you forgot or lost it, you paid up, or there was hell to pay.

The Herbert Strutt Grammar School was opened in 1909 and is a beautiful stone building beside the A6, just outside Belper. Opposite is the Babington Hospital, a massive Victorian edifice, originally a workhouse (though I was unaware of this at the time) designed by George Gilbert Scott. Clearly it was thought that the school should be built in the same style. Certainly it had atmosphere – much of it, during the winter months at any rate, extremely chilly – but it was a pretty impressive place to go to school, with the walls of its great hall covered with polished boards showing former pupils' academic achievements. (Yours truly was not, alas, to be thus exhibited.) Many of the staff wore gowns, and for ceremonial occasions, all did. Even the caretaker had a few letters after his name.

Babington Hospital, which dates from 1840, is now once more under threat of closure, and the school is now the Strutts Community Centre. Even though not everything that happened at school was necessarily a happy experience for everyone, most of it was good, and I for one have very happy memories. It seems to have instilled loyalty in most of us, and I think we would have chained ourselves to the railings gladly if they'd threatened to demolish it.

Belper itself was a revelation. Coming from uptight Allestree to no-holds-barred Belper was something of a culture shock. Suddenly we were on the edge of a world of mills and cobbled streets, rattle-clack voices and funny French surnames, where girls in curlers and headscarves marched four abreast along the streets on seven-inch heels. And the school was just as alien as well. Someone – maybe it was me – once said you could sort the Strutts teachers into just two categories: the saints and the psychopaths. Maybe a slight exaggeration, but I suppose it's only the more exotic ones we tend to remember…

Our first-year form teacher was a Miss Clarke, who wore strange colour combinations, including red-and-yellow socks with sandals. She was young and friendly, and also wore a gown much of the time. I have a feeling she taught Scripture. The forms then still had Greek names, which we rather liked, and began with 2, since originally there had been a preparatory class of some sort. Now there was no first form. All very traditional. My form was 2 Gamma, the form for the youngest intake of the scholastic year. There was only one other pupil in it from our junior school, and he was a boy. Luckily, one that I knew and was on affable terms with at least, but everyone else was a complete stranger. Our room was Room 10, just off the hall.

Our second-year form teacher, Form 3 Alpha, was Mr Appleyard, known as Tommy after a character in a TV serial, tall, bespectacled and benign, who taught French. Then after that, in the third year, Form 4 Alpha, came Mr Gorgeous Jones. Mr Jones – Dr Jones, strictly speaking – was young and dark and very Welsh and almost ridiculously good-looking. With brooding dark eyes, pale skin, slightly aquiline features and thick, wavy black hair, and, of course, A Voice, it was difficult to keep our eyes off him. Lustful teenage glances shot up at him from under every desk lid, a fact of which I suspect he was not entirely unaware and clearly slightly embarrassed about. More than a touch of the Ivor Novellos, minus the camp, made him veer slightly towards a mild form of sarcasm, which usually failed to have much effect, *Ooh, sir, we don't mind* you *telling us off* being the unspoken female response. I dare say some of the boys quite liked him as well. He was always rather formal with us all, referring to us as Mr or Miss Whatever, as if in an attempt to keep us at arm's length. I think he taught maths, but to be honest, I wasn't really paying that much attention. An attractive Welshman is a lovesome thing. He gained his PhD during his first year at the school, and moved on after only a couple of terms, to greater things. Or maybe just to go into a monastery. Black armbands were worn for some time.

It would appear from my school report book – studded, you'll be saddened to know, with 'Could do betters'– that Mr Gorgeous Jones (Dr Jones, Strictly Speaking) had left us by the summer term of 1958, as the final report is signed M. Granger, our art master, of whom more, alas, later. Surprisingly, perhaps, he did give me a good report. Perhaps he'd remembered that I had come top in art the summer before, although, possibly due to our study of architecture the following year, which I hated, my position in the subject had dropped.

The other school heart-throbs were firstly Mr Prince, who taught sciences and was tall and had a moustache and a mischievous sense of humour. He was very attractive too, but not enough to stop me dropping science after the end of the first year in favour of Latin. He too seemed to have left us quite early on, as he doesn't appear in either school reports or school photos much later. The other, though perhaps less of a heart-throb, but very agreeable nonetheless, was Ray Sendall, the maths master. Ray was slightly older and the one all the mothers tended to cast a kindly eye upon at parents' evenings (mine included). He, too, was dark, looked the way slightly older men really ought to look, and was in fact a thoroughly nice chap. He was a good teacher, too, though failed sadly with me. The trauma of lessons in Belfast English with Sir Smyth all those years earlier had finished me as a mathematician for life. Even my dad, patient as he was, had given up. Ray soon realised that trying to teach me the gentle art of mathematics was like trying to teach a wombat to knit a suit of chain mail, though he didn't put it quite so poetically. However, when it came to O Level time, he did inform my parents quite categorically that I didn't have "a snowball in hell's chance" of passing, and allowed me to revise other subjects during his set revision time, if I so wished. You have to respect a man who can admit defeat. I emerged with six out of seven O Levels. My only failure was maths, for which I think I was given the princely mark of 5%, probably for remembering to write my name on the paper.

The other memorable male teachers were Norman Robinson, our wonderful and greatly loved geography teacher, who looked like Peter Sellers and talked a bit like the chattier half of *Wallace and Gromit*. He had a store of highly entertaining stories, ranging from his early teaching experiences in the East End of London, where, he claimed, children were sewn into their clothes for the winter, to strange exploits during the Second World War (mainly funny, but on occasions shocking, too), and was possibly one of the finest teachers and nicest people I've ever come across. It was Norman who instilled in me the love of geography and geology which I still have, and also of local history, about which he was exceptionally knowledgeable. Every time I test my geographical knowledge, or spot a nice drumlin or glacial moraine, I still murmur, "Thank you, Norman" to this day.

Also highly memorable was Mr Green, another brilliant teacher, who taught Scripture and Latin, though usually in a fairly unconventional way, and probably made us laugh almost as much as Norman did. In Norman's case, if he thought you weren't paying attention, he would peer at you over the top of his Peter Sellers glasses, exerting some kind of magical influence until you did, whereas Mr Green's technique, a trifle more violent, was to sidle up to the nearest metal wastepaper bin and give it a mighty kick, which resounded like Big Ben. He tried this on me, on one occasion, and when I failed to turn a hair, said with mock frigidity, "Brenda, you are *supposed* to jump out of your skin when I do that!"

"I know," I said, "but I saw you coming."

We often suspected that Mr Green, whose first name, as far as we knew, was Michael, was the same Michael Green who wrote that hilarious book *The Art of Coarse Acting*, as his humour was very similar and he was, in fact, an excellent actor, but were disappointed to discover it was actually written by someone entirely different. After a year or two, he left, which was a pity, as his place was filled by someone a lot less colourful, and I was saddened to learn, a long time afterwards, from Norman Robinson, as it happened, that he had died quite young.

Also more than worthy of a mention was Mr Quest, who was, I think, the first person to encourage me as a writer. Mr Quest was a quiet but kindly young teacher with fair curly hair, whose acquaintance I first made when he threw me out of the library for messing around. (I don't think I was doing anything particularly naughty, just plaiting my hair or something, but I was supposed to be *studying*, for goodness' sake.) Anyway, at that stage he was not our English teacher, but became so the following year, when he took me under his wing. I had soon got bored with writing conventional essays and instead contributed a parody of a TV western, which was something very popular at the time and really made him laugh. Years later, I revisited this idea, and wrote one, together with naughty lyrics (thanks, Dad), as a Christmas show at Derby Playhouse. I'm sorry neither Mr Quest nor my dad could see it, though I suspect Norman may have done. Mr Quest realised, of course, that I was capable of writing seriously as well, and did his best to encourage me. I only wish more teachers had done the same. Typically, he, too, left after only a year as our English teacher, and I greatly missed him.

To be honest, I can't say I was ever greatly enamoured with any of our female teachers. Miss Asher, one of the young art teachers, who tended to come and go with the rapidity of football managers at Derby County, was nice and gave me good reports. She seems to have been the last female art teacher who taught me, since I dropped the subject after passing my O Level exam with distinction and winning the Arts Prize for my year in 1960. The reasons for this, as well as the frequent changes in the Art Department, may be revealed later. The other nice female teacher was Miss Rudd, who was our music teacher. Miss Rudd was a kind and gentle soul who should never have taken up teaching in the first place, as the kids, especially the boys, gave her hell. I was horrified to read of her, not long ago, in a biography of (Sir) Alan Bates, one of our most famous ex-pupils, in which she is described as a ferocious woman who *bullied the pupils into submission*, since I'm afraid the situation was totally reversed and whoever allowed that statement to go into print should have checked his sources properly. Presumably, he simply confused her with another teacher, but it stands as an unfortunate slur on a very gentle woman. If there's one thing I regret about my time at Strutts, it's the way the pupils treated Miss Rudd.

Miss Simister was the senior mistress, and more than a little formidable, but an excellent English teacher who taught us Shakespeare in the most memorable way. You did not cross her path lightly, however. Equally formidable was another English teacher, also very good at her job, but just a wee bit lacking in the human sympathy department, and whose favourite tactic, if one member of the class had done something to offend her, was to keep the whole lot of us behind till four o'clock and wait until she heard the buses leave before letting us go, whether it was a cold, dark winter's night or no. This may not have been much skin off the noses of those who lived in Belper, but for those of us who lived eight miles or so away, it meant a long, cold and occasionally difficult journey home. I somehow don't think this sort of practice would be looked upon kindly today. In the first year, our English teacher was a Canadian lady on exchange, a Mrs McKeegan, who was large and loud and very pleasant, but I sometimes had difficulty in following what she was saying, as her accent was so strong.

Possibly the most formidable of all was Miss Saull, the French mistress, who mercifully did not teach me all the way through the school, although this turned out, in the end, to put me at a serious disadvantage. Large, grey and lumbering, her nickname was Tusker. Miss Saull's style of teaching consisted of a great deal of shrieking, flapping and twittering, mainly in French, with questions fired at some hapless individual like machine-gun fire, mainly accompanied by the words "*Vite, vite, vite!*" Maybe this technique worked for some – she was considered to be a very good teacher – but to me it was simply a source of irritation and intimidation. (Possibly she was the teacher whom Bates' biographer confused with the unfortunate Miss Rudd.) At any rate, in today's parlance, I'd probably have thought, *Oh for God's sake, get a grip, woman!* But as it was, being shrieked, flapped and twittered at by someone like a gigantic budgie on steroids simply made me shrink. I was quite a shy girl, not used to being shrieked at, and when I finally made it into her class in the sixth form, having been in a class where I'd usually been top, but clearly at a lower standard, Miss Saull simply ignored me. *Takes no part in class* was her single heart-warming comment on my report. From being at the top of the class, I rapidly plunged to the bottom.

The other totally terrifying female teacher, whom my friend Sandra described as "the most savage woman I've ever met," was Miss Pooley, the domestic science mistress. Miss Pooley was a Lowland Scot, young and thin and exceedingly foul-tempered, her habit of standing behind you with a sharpened carving knife or pair of well-honed scissors in her hand being distinctly worrying. Someone has since suggested that Puddles, as she was known, may have been as frightened of us as we were of her, but perhaps that's being a little overgenerous. She certainly terrified me, and put Sandra off domestic issues for life. I remember the first thing she expected us to make was Welsh rarebit, and to do this, she told us to make the mixture, then slap the whole runny mess onto a slice of untoasted bread and then shove it under the grill. I may have been only eleven, but it struck me immediately that Miss Pooley was out of her tree. My cookery lessons were strangely ill-fated, and on one occasion, I remember a bag of sugar for cake-making revealed, when poured into the scale pan, a large dead fly squashed flat at the bottom. Presumably it had got in there during packaging and was nothing to do with me. I kept quiet and dropped it hastily into the bin. On another occasion, bearing in mind that Tupperware pots and other closable plastic containers were not in general circulation at the time so we had to make do with casserole dishes, a whole stew overturned into the bottom of my cookery basket on the bus. I didn't mention that, either. I just shovelled it up, fluff and all, and carried on home. Everybody ate it. Nobody noticed.

That sort of thing, plus the weekly nightmare of frantic phone-calling the night before between classmates, for ingredients which had been forgotten or were unobtainable, followed by the verbal abuse from Miss P the following day if we hadn't got them all, was beginning to tell on my nerves. And not just mine, either. Pupils knocked off sick and mothers blanched at the very mention of domestic science lessons. Not only cookery, but sewing lessons were a nightmare too, and I finally finished my cookery apron, our task for the first year, three years after I left. Strangely enough, I have only just learned, after years of getting it wrong, that Miss Pooley, whom I'd always assumed to be a Lowland Scot, was not a mad Scotswoman after all, but a mad Cumbrian. But I always knew she was perilously close to the border.

Miss Pooley's constant goading and knife- or scissor-wielding got on my nerves so badly that I eventually vowed some form of vengeance. I spent a great deal of time during sewing lessons cutting the heads off pins, or simply dropping them all and picking them up very slowly. My pièce de résistance, however – and Sandra dined out on this one for years – was slowly and deliberately filling all the gas jets on the cookers with Vim after being obliged to stay behind and clean them for some minor misdemeanour. Boy, did I do a good job. The hoped-for explosion did not occur, but the room was out of action for a week. (Clearly, it never occurred to me how dangerous this practice could have been. *Do not do this at home, children.* Or indeed, anywhere else.) After this, my methods of Pooley-baiting became more subtle. I knuckled down, worked really hard and came top in the exam. It was too much for Miss P. At the end of the summer term, she emigrated to Canada and was never seen again. As a footnote, however, I have to add, my friend Eileen went one better. She knuckled down, went on to college, and became a domestic science teacher.

The other principle psycho was our form master for 1958–59, one Horace Grenville, an enigmatic soul to say the least. Mr Grenville taught biology and was also in charge of the school's army cadet force. Gren, as he was known, could be affable and amusing one minute, then fly off the handle to earth-shattering effect the next. On one occasion (and I have no idea what this was all about), he banged his fist on the desk so hard that it bled, shouting and yelling until his face was like an apoplectic tomato; and on another he slammed the classroom door till it split from top to bottom. I, personally, never fell out with him, but anyone who did was in for a highly memorable experience, which usually involved everyone else in the vicinity as well. A Grenville tantrum could be heard several miles away.

Someone told me, years later at a reunion, that Gren was a Polish Jew, though I did not pursue this line of enquiry, nor did I like the way in which it was said. Perhaps it was more of a personal grudge against Gren – not difficult, really, bearing in mind his temper – rather than a touch of anti-Semitism, but I must say that I was surprised, as Gren spoke impeccable public-school English. An incident with a swastika doodle someone had foolishly drawn sprang to mind. Probably there was a lot more to his story than any of us knew. Whatever it might have been, he was perfectly fair and benevolent towards me, and I've come across more than one war-damaged personality since then and know how quickly their moods can swing. Hazy stories relating to the War still permeated through the strata of our lives in some ways, especially regarding a couple of the female teachers, alleged to have lost fiancés during the conflict, but again, whether this was true or simply the scholastic equivalent of the urban legend, I shall never know.

One other teacher worthy (if that's the word – well, no, in the circumstances, perhaps not) was Dixie, a big, balding, brooding man with a resonant voice and a beady stare. Dixie, it was, as far as I recall, who replaced the sympathetic and benevolent Mr Quest, and taught English and Scripture. Dixie, and we'll leave it at that for ID purposes, came with an interesting reputation, having been allegedly an unfrocked vicar/priest/Nonconformist minister (take your pick), and shortly after his arrival was involved in a mildly scandalous divorce case. Well, he made it into the papers, anyway. He also had a run-in with a malevolent landlady who threw all his possessions out into the street, which also made it into the papers. Naturally, this was excellent gossip fodder for teenage pupils, who loved every minute of it. However, on the credit side, I have to say, Dixie's problems seemed to be with grown-up ladies, and he didn't abuse kids. To be fair, he wasn't a bad teacher, either.

Dixie lived to a great age, having achieved that sort of assumed sanctity people seem to achieve once they pass the eighty mark, and for a while actually had the honour of being the oldest man in the UK. I last spoke to him at a school reunion, shortly before the school closed for good, although I doubt very much that he remembered who I was, which was perhaps just as well, since some years earlier, assuming he'd long since gone on to his reward, I'd written an article mentioning the above brouhaha, and was mortified to discover that he hadn't. Dixie belonged to a local male voice choir for many years, and when I once mentioned to someone, at an event long after his death, that I knew him, they shuffled uncomfortably and changed the subject. Poor Dixie's reputation evidently lasted even longer than he did.

NINETEEN

Growing Up a Bit
(Though Not a Lot...)

I always enjoyed the journey to school, apart from days when I hadn't done my homework or a hockey lesson was nigh. As we rounded Burley Hill, I still looked for The House That Wasn't There, but it still wasn't there. Once we passed Duffield, the scenery began to change. It was always good to see that first green glimpse of the Chevin shining in the sun. In winter, great rolls of mist, like Shredded Wheat, lay in the valley between the river and the railway. There was Moscow Farm, so named as it was built in 1812, then the Strutt Arms at Milford, where I would later go to the jazz club on occasions, and opposite the pub, a curious set of stone terraces, almost overgrown, which I later learned had been constructed as an intended vineyard many years before, but the Derwent Valley climate had defeated them. Now covered by modern housing, you would never know they had ever been there.

By the time we got into the second year (which, in Strutts parlance, was the third form; in my case, 3 Alpha), proper friendships were established after that slightly uneasy first year. I became friends with Sandra, from the small village of Sawmills just outside Ambergate, and even though we lost touch for many years after leaving school, we eventually met up again in the 1990s and became best friends once more. Sandra was taller than me, with pale skin and freckles, black hair, cat-like, emerald-green eyes, and a daft sense of humour. Even-tempered and inclined to be self-effacing, she was exactly the same easy-going, unaffected person at fifty-two that she'd been at twelve, and I never met anyone who didn't like her. Sandra died some years ago and I still miss her.

Also in our class was Liz, even taller, who lived in Allestree, but had, I think, gone to the village school. We three hung about together during class time. Then there was the aforementioned Eileen, who was in a different class, and was therefore a part-time member of our little set, having another of her own, but as she also lived in Allestree, she and I often met up in the evenings and holidays. Eileen lived in an ancient farmhouse, just round the corner from where Mrs Brocklehurst loomed over her tiny counter like a slag heap in a dress. Even Eileen had never encountered the mysterious Mr Brocklehurst, aka Brock the Clown, so maybe he had already gone off to work for Stephen King. Eileen's mum was also large, but a sylph compared to Mrs Brock, and affable enough in that "Ooh, look at that sky, we'll pay for this in the morning" sort of way beloved of most farmers' wives. Her dad was seldom sighted, other than leaning on a gate, staring morosely into the distance. The farmyard was occupied by an unruly mob of geese, possibly the most ferocious creatures I've ever met, and even Eileen was scared of them.

Eileen was small and busty and very good company, at least until something in trousers appeared, in which case she tended to be off like a short but well-stacked gazelle, but she was great fun to be with. In fact, Eileen was as small, bold and flirty as Liz was tall, prim and reserved, and I don't remember the three of us hanging about together much out of school, for fear of possible embarrassment – to Liz, rather than to me or Eileen – so I went around with one or the other, but not usually both at the same time. Liz's parents were older than mine, and, although pleasant, seemed rather formal and austere, whereas Eileen's were more laissez-faire. I suppose mine came somewhere in the middle. Liz's father was a headmaster, while Sandra's parents were both factory workers, so we were quite a mixed bag. Sandra, of course, lived much too far away for regular out-of-school meetings, but we did sometimes manage to meet up during the school holidays.

Eileen had two other close friends, both from the Belper area or beyond: Pauline, who told us her grandfather had been a German Jew, thus making her on the verge of slightly exotic, and who was also from a farming family, and Carol, about whom I knew very little. Pauline seemed ordinary enough at twelve but abruptly turned into a real beauty at fifteen or sixteen, with dark golden hair and big brown eyes, and when I met her at a reunion in the 1990s, I think she had married a farmer. Carol was possibly even naughtier than Eileen, and usually had a distinct tidemark of pinkish-orange make-up around her neck, and, whenever possible, wore a transparent blouse (how she got away with these transgressions under the eagle eye of Miss Simister and co. I'll never know), and talked like Amanda Barrie in *Carry On Cleo*. I've no idea what happened to her.

Evenings out with Eileen were never dull. We would often go to Allestree Park together, or walk around Darley Abbey, sometimes to gaze at the impressive house of some sixth-former we were keen on. Opposite the Court Cafe was some farmland, down a steep incline from the road, and we would sit there on a low stone wall, the top of which only just raised above the pavement. There were some curious cattle shelters, set into an overhanging bank further down, which always reminded me of the stable at Bethlehem. A little further on, closer to Darley Abbey, lived a boy Eileen went out with for a while, though this must have been later. On one occasion, she managed to drop her purse over the low wall and down into the field below, which must have been a drop of six feet or so. We simply couldn't reach it. While we were upended like ducks on a pond, some innocent young lad came by and Eileen re-reversed and said, very politely, "Excuse me, but have you got a piece of string with a hook on the end?", to which he bleated some feeble excuse and beat a very hasty retreat, possibly unnerved by the sight of two female rears so blatantly revealed. I can't remember how we retrieved the purse in the end, but we did. I think I must have held on to her ankles.

On another occasion, while adventuring on the golf course side of Allestree Park, Eileen managed to sit in Something Nasty, and found to her horror that not only did she smell bad, but she was being pursued by a swarm of flies. With a piercing shriek, she whipped off her jeans, chucked them over her arm and ran for home, via a barbed-wire fence (not wise), still pursued by the flies, in a pair of bright green and very brief pants. Luckily, she knew a shortcut back to the farm from there, and was off over the next barbed-wire fence and a gate like a supercharged cheetah and into the farmyard, followed by the flies and, of course, the geese, who had a penchant for varnished toenails *and* bright green pants, evidently. By this time, I was laughing so much, I had to go straight home before my own pants, which I'm sure were the more demure, navy blue Strutts School-approved variety, complete with gusset, required attention too. As I said, life with Eileen was never dull.

Liz, on the other hand, was rather more formal, and less likely to have run around Allestree in bright green knickers, although I'm not sure quite how she (or I, for that matter) would have dealt with that particular situation.

Sometime around the Christmas of our second year, my grandfather was taken seriously ill, and my mother went over to Normanton to help look after him. On the night of the school Christmas party, Liz's mother very kindly offered to let me stay there, so that no one from home would have to come and collect me. Two things I remember in particular. One was that the family always said grace before commencing a meal (unexpected by little heathens like Eileen, Sandra and myself), and the other was the crocodile on top of the wardrobe. Apparently the family had lived in Egypt for a while, long before Liz was born, and the stuffed crocodile was a souvenir from there, but it was a little unnerving. Strangely enough, when we met in later life, although she smiled while remembering the grace, Liz claimed to have completely forgotten the crocodile, which I would have thought to have been highly memorable. I certainly never met anyone else who had one.

Visits between myself and Sandra were fairly rare, as it required either two or three different buses, depending on how energetic you were feeling, to reach each other. However, we did try to meet up at least once during the summer holidays, but the journey tended to take up half the day. I remember her staying with us once or twice, but we didn't have a spare room and neither did they, and since my grandfather sadly died following that Christmas illness, my grandmother spent some time living with us too. No more would Grandpa's pre-

War black Standard 10, CRA 618, or its successor, the silver-grey Triumph Mayflower, pull up outside our gate. A kind and gentle man; I missed him.

As soon as Grandma returned to her own home, my cousin Tessa became very ill, and my mother was called upon to look after her, so my room was taken up again. I think, at this time, I may have had to sleep in the lounge or my parents' room on a folding bed, as she was deemed highly infectious, and I remember my mother having to burn handkerchiefs and tissues outside in the yard. All this occurred almost as soon as we had left a three-bedroom house for a two-bed one. Tess had been at teacher training college and had to take a year out, though she did eventually go back and qualify. The story went that she got locked out one night after coming back very late from a party and no one would let her in. It was freezing cold, and she ended up with pneumonia and rheumatic fever. This was what had killed my grandmother's sister all those years earlier, and not something to be taken lightly.

The next casualty was me. First with chickenpox, then with a broken ankle, having jumped out of a tree and landed a mite too heavily. Or it may have been the other way round. Either way, I missed two sizeable chunks of school, both in summer or spring terms, when I regret to say I lounged around listening to the radio and eating sweets all day and putting on weight. My mother had taken a job as a part-time music teacher by this time, and so was not at home long enough to keep an eye on me, and while I was never grossly overweight, it took me a long time to shed those extra pounds.

The other sad thing was that our beloved dog died. He was fourteen years old and I missed him terribly. He was eventually replaced by a dizzy blonde collie cross called Peggy, she of turkey-fat-gobbling fame, found wandering among heavy traffic on Swarkestone Bridge, that ancient mile-long causeway across the Trent, and rescued by a kindly lorry driver who took her to the RSPCA. Peggy was a naughty dog compared to Ruffy, at least to begin with, and had a tendency to run off, which presumably is how she got lost in the first place. She also had a tendency to round things up, like sheep, cattle, anything on legs, really; as we discovered to our horror, the first time she slipped her lead. She wasn't aggressive towards livestock, she just liked to set them in order, but try telling that to a farmer with a shotgun. Luckily, we managed to retrain her before any damage was done, and as she was actually a very sweet-natured dog, we soon became friends. She was also befriended by our Scottish neighbour, and every time he got his car out, she would hop onto the passenger seat beside him. Viewed from behind, with her floppy golden ears above the seat back, she looked like a young blonde woman, and was soon referred to as Mr Brown's girlfriend. Like Ruffy, she lived to a good old age.

I was relieved to have got into the second year at Strutts and established myself with a couple of good friends during class and afterwards. Occasionally, travelling on the school bus could be a bit hairy until Eileen and Liz joined me further along the way, since the BVM of dirty phone call fame had, for some reason best known to herself, started some kind of petty vendetta against me, coupled with my former friend Margaret, though luckily, after a while, they seemed to lose interest. However, I wouldn't pretend there wasn't an element of malice aimed in my direction occasionally. On the way home, we usually sat downstairs, whereas they sat upstairs, to avoid any further confrontations. On the whole, though, I never encountered much in the way of bullying at Strutts, although a bit of verbal viciousness came my way from time to time. Much of it seemed to be centred around my name, which certain people found amusing – I've never quite understood the English obsession with that sort of trivia, really. While I know it's fun to concoct suitable names, especially if you're a writer – one Charles Dickens tended to go a bit OTT with this one – it never seems to occur to anyone that in real life, there is an actual human being behind the name, and it might be a good idea to find out what they're really like before slinging the mud. There could be an interesting person there, for all they know. I changed my professional name when I started writing, and changed it again when I married, and that's how it has stayed.

Strutts had quite a strict uniform policy at the time we were there, at least as far as the girls were concerned, and transgressions were usually dealt with swiftly and sharply. However, this did not prevent the Eileens and Carols among us from trying it on, and sometimes the results could be highly entertaining. One of the fashions of the mid 1950s was the hooped underskirt – the hoop being a narrow band of plastic threaded through a horizontal seam halfway down. The effect of anyone sitting down or bending over in one of these was hilarious, since as one end went down, the other shot up, revealing all. Assuming that anyone could actually cram one of these under a school dress (under a straight or slightly flared school skirt, it was virtually impossible, but being Eileen or Carol, you had to try, obviously), the results were spectacular. Luckily for us, Brigitte Bardot had made the gingham dress, the school dictate of summer wear, fashionable, and the illicit hooped underskirt was a godsend to the eyes of every passing male. Getting a school blazer over the top as well tended to make the wearer look like a half-open umbrella, but for the few short hours before you were caught, it was worth it. The Belperites caught thus sinning were no doubt sent home to change, whereas those from further afield were doomed to shove the offending garment as best they could into a locker like a partially deflated barrage balloon until four o'clock.

Strangely enough, the uniform rules seemed much slacker as far as the boys were concerned, despite the fact that the senior master and his successor were, frankly, a bit sadistic. String ties and shoulder pads were frequently worn, school blazers miraculously became 'Ted' jackets, and rules were flouted in other ways. Weird haircuts seemed to escape notice and purges were only occasional. While it had not escaped my notice that girls from richer families seemed to get away with things like fancy buttons on garments, posh shoes and occasional hair ornaments, bolder deviations were quickly frowned upon, whereas the boys got away with so much more. How little things change…

Frankly, my parents didn't have enough ready cash to blow on modifying my school uniform in the direction of current fashion, and were not awfully happy to discover that said uniform was only available from a very expensive shop in Belper, with no deviations (unless you were somehow ultra-privileged, it would appear), and while I'm in favour of uniforms in general, they need to be a leveller, not a symbol of prestige, which rather goes against the point. Hearing of children in earlier days whose parents had to turn down their places at grammar schools simply because they couldn't afford the uniform makes me truly angry. Clothes had not been rationed since 1949, but they were certainly not cheap. I remember Sandra telling me that her mother said, having acquired her first (and only) set of uniform, "Don't you dare grow! This is the only lot you're getting!" Yes, I know how she felt.

Even when my own children started at secondary school, much the same rules existed, until, a year after we had squandered money on uniforms, the local authority decided the wearing of them was elitist or undemocratic and abandoned the practice altogether, much to our fury. Even after this, a great deal of nitpicking went on about what should or shouldn't be worn, making me wish some kind of national policy could be settled once and for all, with the required garments made as cheap and available as possible. To be fair, our own school uniform wasn't unattractive, being navy blue, light blue and white, unlike that of a rival grammar school which opened a couple of years later, whose unfortunate pupils were condemned to wear a hideous shade of magenta. All in all, I wasn't unhappy with it. The '50s were a tacky time, fashion-wise, so perhaps being obliged to wear a uniform for a few years wasn't such a bad thing.

Looking at old photographs, it seems as though real style had lasted till the outbreak of the Second World War but had become tired and faded by the end of it, when it was replaced by the awful artificiality of the New Look. On the whole, the '50s were either stiff and formal or floppy and formal, and, apart from a few teenage fashions that had filtered in from France or the US, fashion wasn't really fun till the '60s got under way. And I wouldn't have missed that for the world!

TWENTY

Mud, Blood and Hockey

Some years ago, I was having breakfast in a small hotel in Cardiff with my husband when we got chatting to a big, burly bloke who was the manager of a men's hockey team from Ireland. After he'd finished extolling the virtues and manliness of the game, I asked him if he'd ever heard of a small town called Belper, in Derbyshire, where said game was played by strong women in mud up to their knees, the like of which rivalled something in a Roman arena for violence. He didn't seem awfully impressed. When we saw him again in the evening, I asked if they'd won. "No," he replied, with just a hint of irony. "We came second."

Hockey in the Belper mud was not something you'd joke about. Not if you cared for life and limb, anyway. It was something you hid from. Our sports field was over the road from the school, adjacent to the grounds of Babington Hospital, and sloped slightly down towards the River Derwent. They were lovely playing fields in summer, with tennis courts and a cricket pitch surrounded by shady trees, but in winter, when they were turned into hockey and football pitches, they became a sea of mud, occasionally scattered with pockets of ice. The hard tennis court also doubled as a netball court, but I honestly don't ever remember playing netball there. Perhaps it was simply too ladylike for the young women of Belper. I was quite good at tennis – the only sport I actually enjoyed, although I could run and jump a bit – but ironically, none of my friends liked tennis, so apart from actual lessons, my tennis-playing usually had to take place away from school. Hockey, on the other hand, was another matter. A bloodbath in a mudbath was probably the best way to describe it, and giving any girl from Belper a weapon as lethal as a hockey stick was definitely tempting fate.

Having established my relative uselessness early on, yours truly and another girl, Val, were always relegated to the position of goalkeeper, not because we had any talent whatever in that direction, but simply because we were always the ones left over once teams had been chosen. Val said she used to spend her time leaning against the goalpost, watching the planes going over from Manchester or old Derby Airport, later to be replaced by East Midlands International, and thinking, *Ooh, I wish I was up there…* I just shivered by the goal at the opposite end, hoping no fast-moving ball or violently wielded stick would come my way and keeping an eye peeled for any passing talent on the adjacent football pitch, which, if it was our year playing, would be pretty unlikely, since they were not a very desirable lot. I do have a vague memory of Mr Prince taking the occasional football lesson. There was always hope.

The actual games master was Mr Johnson, or Johnstone, one of several Johnny Johnsons who had some connection with *The Dam Busters*, although not, apparently, the last surviving pilot of that name, as I seem to remember reading an article about him years ago saying that he was a back-room boy involved in planning the raid. He was a balding, red-faced, cheery sort of man, loud of voice, and the only time I ever remember him speaking (or rather shouting) to me was when I fell in the mud during a particularly valiant (and uncharacteristic) save, and he bellowed, "Get up, girl, don't just lie there!" It was probably my finest moment on the hockey field. Normally, the hockey and football instructors did not overlap in their duties, so perhaps the hockey mistress had gone to the loo, or simply been diverted by the more alluring sight of Mr Prince. On looking at the old school photo from 1959, I seem to recognise a Mr Price, as well, who I think may have been an assistant games master. He wasn't bad-looking, either, so may have been another possible diversion.

The sports mistress was the strangely named Mrs Banderis, a stocky, dark-haired woman, who would have been good-looking had she not possessed a perpetual thunderous scowl. Usually referred to as Bandy, she was not over-popular, even with those who were good at games. She had a tongue like a whiplash and seemed to suffer from permanent PMT. Goading pupils to greater heights, or, in the case of hockey in the mud, depths, with penetrating shrieks of sarcasm, seemed to be her one activity, and I never remember her exerting herself unduly as she lounged around in her nice warm tracksuit, while we shivered in shorts. Bearing in mind that she was quite young, not unattractive and probably had a reasonably desirable job, I'm not sure what it was that made her so sour. Things came to a head one day when one of the senior boys chucked a javelin at her. This occurred after some event and was not quite as violent as it sounds, since he actually only slid it very fast along the ground in the direction of her foot, but it could have caused a nasty injury had she not jumped out of the way in time. The boy – and I do know who it was but discretion forbids – was severely yelled at by other staff present, but strangely, no one ever heard any more about it. Needless to say, rightly or wrongly, the javelin thrower became the hero of the day. On the whole, I have to say, games, at least in winter, were not my favourite lessons.

Occasionally, when it was deemed too icy for hockey or possibly too foggy to see the ball, we would be dispatched on a long walk, either over the lower slopes of the Chevin, usually pitted with snow, or around the backwaters of the town, which was unknown territory to we non-Belperites and often proved interesting. I remember seeing the remains of the old nail-makers' workshops, which was one of the town's main occupations before the mills arrived. However, as I grew older, I discovered that it *was* possible to escape from games lessons in the infamous Belper mud, and by the time I'd got into the sixth form, when the whole year took their session together and missing pupils became less obvious, it had become an art. It was then, lurking in the alcoves of the school library, that my first serious steps as a writer began.

Looking again at that school photograph, which was one of those massive efforts printed on an endless roll, I seem to recognise another teacher who also appeared briefly on the hockey field, the aptly named Miss Sturdy. She doubled as one of the fast-coming, fast-going art mistresses, and I doubt she lasted the year out. Missing from this picture seems to be Fred West (no, not *that* Fred West – ours was a nice guy who lived in Allestree and taught maths, though was lucky enough not to get landed with me), and another art mistress who put in a couple of years before departing with the usual haste. This one, who must have preceded the friendly and encouraging Miss Asher, was quite nice to me at the time, if in a slightly patronising way, and wrote on my report, *Brenda has talent*. Many years later, I encountered her again when I was working in the library service, and said hello and introduced myself, to be greeted by some cuttingly acidic remark of the *Why the hell should I remember some scummy kid like you?* variety, which left me virtually speechless. I felt like saying, *Maybe because I won the O Level Arts Prize for my year, perhaps?*, but refrained, handed her the books, and silently wished her ill fortune. I'm pleased to say she never reappeared.

The reason for the rapid comings and goings of female art teachers would appear to have been the art master, one Mr Granger, a strange, tall, balding, vulture-like character, whose attitude towards the world in general seemed to be one of complete contempt. Mr Granger was certainly interested in girls, but not in ones who were good at art. For some, he would appear to have had a fatal attraction, whereas to Sandra and myself, he was known as Old Camel's Breath. ("And that," as my dad put it, "was why they called him the Lone Granger.") Yet, talking to some of his male pupils years after he had been removed ignominiously from the school, they said what an inspiration he'd been to them. Certainly he did dash all for me. But let's not go there.

I notice that on that school photo, taken in 1959, it is mainly the women teachers who have managed a smile. Even Miss Simister is wearing a half-smirk that looks as though she's just passed a sarky comment to Mr Matthias, who by this time had become headmaster, replacing the benign but remote George Ducker, obliged to retire on grounds of age just before the school celebrated its golden jubilee that year – rather unfairly, everyone thought. In fact, the only male teacher who looks positively cheerful is Johnny Walpole, who taught biology and is wearing a noticeably non-Strutts light jacket and is one of the few teachers not wearing a gown. Next to him is Bryan Chapman, also wearing a light jacket, and renowned for his gaudy colour combinations of red tie and green shirt, or vice versa, which a gown does not quite conceal. He was our form master in the fifth year, and I think he taught physics, so never actually taught me. Even Ray Sendall and Norman Robinson don't look awfully happy. Normally cheerful Mr Green is sunk in gloom and Dixie has his usual penetrating glare. On the pupils' side, I am at the far end, next to the back row, with Eileen just in front of me. For once, I am looking at the camera and actually smiling, and both of us look fairly respectable, although my hair is shorter than I would have liked it. Liz and Sandra are much harder to find, somewhere in the middle.

TWENTY-ONE

Benedictus! Beetroot and Bad Digestion

School dinners at Strutts were unspeakably awful. Since I lived a long way from school, it seemed only sensible to opt for them, at least in the beginning. It was a mistake that I, and almost the whole of the Allestree contingent, would soon regret. Lunch was served in what had (obviously) to be known as the Refectory, a large pre-prefabricated building up a few steps to the right of the main buildings. It was served on long trestle tables and pupils were seated on benches which made the most appalling noise when moved around the floor, which happened, needless to say, every time anyone had to sit down or stand up again. This was not quite as appalling as what preceded the act of sitting down, however. Or indeed, the culinary mayhem that came afterwards.

Before every meal could begin came the ominous ritual of Latin grace. It went something along the lines of:

Benedictus, benedicat
Per Iesum Christum
Dominum Nostrum
Something, something
Amen

That first 'Benedictus' was always drawn out for as long as possible, with much emphasis on the last syllable, after a very lengthy pause, while all assembled waited with bated breath for something to go wrong. It was usually sung by Miss Saull, who had a voice like the *Queen Mary* sailing cautiously into Southampton through heavy fog, and invariably provoked a chorus of barely suppressed hilarity. One always hoped an express heading for Sheffield and places north would belt under the railway bridge at the back of Room 18, drowning her out at the appropriate moment, but sadly one never did. Should Miss Saull not be present, or with luck be suffering from laryngitis, then even more fun was to be had as anxious members of staff could be seen exchanging furtive glances and practically heard muttering, "Well, I'm not going to do it – you do it, I did it last time", etc., as pupils grinned happily and shuffled, waiting for the first quavering attempts of the next sucker to try it. With luck, a kid at the end would fall off a bench, just to liven things up a bit, then finally we were allowed to pitch into whatever horrors the school kitchen had provided. We once asked Mr Green, our Latin teacher, what the 'Benedictus' grace actually meant, and were delighted when he informed us that, strictly speaking, it didn't mean anything; it was just a few Latin words and phrases chucked together to sound impressive and didn't actually make sense at all. But to this day, any former Strutts School pupil of my generation can't hear the word 'Benedictus' without falling about laughing.

To be honest, I simply can't remember (or identify) what the majority of the main courses actually were. They did seem to consist of a lot of potatoes, either as watery mash or bashed around in lumps, and frequently beetroot, which stained the plates, only ever warm if we were having salad, like detritus from an operating theatre. Vaguely I seem to recall squidged cabbage and tepid carrots from time to time, and lumps of gristly meat, sometimes with bits of blue print attached to them. Occasionally, I recall some form of meat pie, which was on the verge of edible. Perhaps it had been made with mince out of a tin. Luckily, Belper in the 1950s had not yet discovered anything as sophisticated as broccoli or courgettes, so loved today by restaurants doing things on the cheap, or we'd have had a load of those as well. Puddings were usually something slab-like to be drenched in custard, or something we took to be semolina, popularly known as Bird Poo, or tapioca, aka Frogspawn, which didn't need further lubrication. On occasions, we would also get with either of these some kind of chocolate-flavoured flapjack, which was actually quite palatable. However, if you were sitting at the far end of the table from the prefect who was doling it out, or she simply didn't like you, you were lucky if you got any. Male and female pupils were segregated, by the way, with a sort of raft of teachers in the middle, but whether this helped in any way, I somehow doubt. I remember us asking Tommy Appleyard, then our form teacher, if he ever stayed for school dinners. "Not if I can possibly help it," came the admirably honest reply.

At the end of the first term, I went down on bended knee and pleaded with my mother to let me take sandwiches, which I did forever after. Sandra's mother, however, clearly less compassionate, refused, and she alone out of our small group was obliged to suffer school dinners for the next five years.

Together with the trauma of being taught domestic science by Miss Pooley, it was enough to blunt her palate and put her off any form of culinary activity for life, or so she claimed. Every day, after we'd finished our packed lunches in Room 18, sniggering sinfully at the distant strains of 'Benedictus' from the Refectory, we used to wait for her to join us, still slightly green around the gills, before making our way to field, quad or whatever classroom or corridor weather permitted. Very often, in winter, we would spend our lunch hours toasting our rears on the radiators in some corridor somewhere until, along with the dust from the hall floor, our navy blue skirts were patterned with fine scorch marks.

Another downside of daily life at Strutts was Assembly. While I'm actually quite in favour of a little non-denominational or non-religious contemplation early in the morning, Assembly could be a bit of a pain in the backside. The main reason for this was that we had to sit on the floor for most of it, leaving our hitherto clean skirts or trousers covered with white dust and footprints for the rest of the day. On the other hand, it was probably better than standing, since George Ducker, our original headmaster, was known for Going On a Bit. His successor, R. G. Matthias, Welshman that he was, although verbose, could at least be quite entertaining. George, however, could drone. Even Miss Simister, on more than one occasion, could be seen to groan and roll her eyes.

Junior Assembly was held for pupils of the first two years, in the gym, and I can't honestly remember who took it. The blessing was that it was slightly shorter than senior Assembly, presumably so that we could get the hell out of it before the older pupils left the hall, but in our case, this was a waste of time, since our classroom led off the hall anyway and thus the usual elbow-jabbing traffic jam ensued. Senior Assembly consisted of a hymn (George's favourite was 'He who would valiant be(To Be a Pilgrim)' and a prayer, followed by the notices, for which we were allowed to sit. Everyone attended Assembly, except for the Roman Catholics, who at this stage in ecclesiastical development were not allowed to attend acts of common worship for fear they should become morally contaminated. They were allowed to stay in a room just off the hall, where they behaved riotously in the care of some unfortunate prefect until the rest of us were released. Also with them were a few unidentified dissenters, several of whom had Russian-sounding names, though whether Orthodox, Marxist or whatever I never found out. The Jewish kids, what few there were, usually just mucked in with the rest of us, who were mainly, I suppose Anglican, or other Protestant Indifferents, pretty well like me. Of other faiths at this time, there simply seemed to be none.

Once a year, in November, at the time closest to Remembrance Sunday, the school held its own Remembrance service, remembering the pupils and staff who had died in both World Wars. Following the service, for which we all stood, their names were read out, followed by a two- or three-minute silence, during which somebody would invariably pass out, hitting the floor with an ominous thud. It was usually a boy. Then, between the gym and the hall, Mr Higgs, the school caretaker (a fine musician, in fact), would play 'The Last Post' on the bugle. It was strangely moving, and we all filed out into the thin autumn sunlight greatly sobered.

The gym had apparently been the original refectory, and not long before we began at the school, the prefab refectory had been built and a room above the newly installed gymnasium had been created to make the Memorial Library, as a tribute to those lost staff and pupils. On the wall opposite one of the long tables there was a large wooden plaque bearing their names. At the very bottom of the list was a single girl. I was always intrigued by this, and often when sitting there, my eyes would look up and focus on her name and I wondered what had happened to her. Quite by chance, a few years after I left, I found out, and later wrote a fictionalised story about her. It was called *Rosalie Jane*.[5] That was not her real name, of course, but she was the daughter of a friend of my grandmother's, she came from the village of Crich not far away, and apparently she looked like me.

---

5   In *The Siren of Salamanca*.

TWENTY-TWO

And Also...

Strutts was a large school, at least by 1950s standards, so there were, of course, a lot of teachers there who never taught me at all. On looking again at that 1959 photo, there are quite a few that I simply don't recognise. Since I chose to do Latin and arts and dropped sciences altogether the year before O Levels, I never really knew the science teachers, apart from Gren and Mr Chapman, both of whom were our form masters. The senior history master, Roland Sutton, I scarcely knew, as by the time he was supposed to be teaching us, he had become quite elderly and was absent a lot due to failing health. He was memorable for having written the words to the school song. (George Ducker had written the music.) I remember him mainly as an elderly man with white hair and a bright yellow forelock, which I naively assumed must have been its original colour. Someone later informed me that it was simply nicotine.

There were other people who were either support staff or on the periphery of teaching, such as lab assistants, and part-timers who were only seen occasionally, including a music teacher called Mrs Walker, a large lady who knew my mother (alas) through various school music functions, where they no doubt discussed my inadequacy in that field with a resigned sigh, and an annual French mam'zelle, invariably pretty and very charming, who set male hearts of all ages aflutter. One of these ladies was very taken with a boy in our class, and vice versa (he was quite nice-looking), and would always home in on him, possibly with deliberate mischief in mind, and ask him where he lived, beginning with "Ah, Monsieur Dickie...", which was how he'd introduced himself, and ask him where he lived, to be rewarded, accompanied by much blushing and eyelash-dipping, with the happily anticipated phrase "*J'habite à Openwoodgate.*" It never failed to get a laugh.

Also worthy of mention is Miss Carr, not so much because of anything she actually did, but for the atmosphere that surrounded her, which hit you rather like the blast you get when you open the door of a hot oven. In Miss Carr's case it wasn't heat that hit you, but a waft of something called Coty L'Aimant, a sickly enough scent at the best of times, but when applied in copious doses – or possibly, though I hate to say it, never actually washed off – you could tell when she had passed by within a time lag of ten minutes or more, even if you hadn't actually seen her. Miss Carr was a tall, slim blonde with a pudding-basin haircut, wont to wear rather a lot of pinkish-orange make-up and ornate, heavy-rimmed spectacles, and frequently seen in the company of Mr Cumbers, the senior Classics master. Rumours always seemed to abound about this relationship, which I suspect was actually perfectly innocent, but fifteen-year-olds have suspicious minds. Neither of them ever taught me. But any girl who ever attended Strutts, on approaching the perfume counter in a large store, would always give Coty L'Aimant a very wide berth indeed.

I don't remember Mr Cumbers particularly well, apart from his being tall, thin and balding, with a small expanse of hair either side of his baldness, and otherwise unmemorable. There were a number of male teachers who went into this particular bracket, were covered by the same approximate description, and seemed to have had much the same personality bypass. Perhaps I'm being mean here, and prejudiced by the fact that none of them ever taught me, or I would have remembered them. There were also a couple of elderly, white-haired, bleating ones who may or may not have had spindly beards, both of whom did teach me, and seem to have been relatively harmless as well as a bit ineffectual, and were, in my mind, completely interchangeable. Perhaps the women were more memorable simply because there were fewer of them. And as far as I remember, none of them had a beard, but perhaps I'm being too kind.

Another miscellaneous character was Miss Terry, the head's secretary, a tall, bespectacled lady with a nervous twitch and strange, jerky movements who may have had some kind of neurological condition. Yet another was our caretaker, Mr Higgs, or 'Mr 'Iggs', in Belper parlance, who was a small, surprised-looking man in dungarees with a remarkable resemblance to Bugs Bunny. He, it was, who played the bugle at Remembrance Day services, and very well, too. His son, I believe, became a professional musician. Then there was Mrs Matt.

Quite what Mrs Matt's exact position on the Strutts staff was, I am a little uncertain, but I think today she might have been categorised as a school welfare officer, although what kind of welfare she actually performed is open to debate. Mrs Matt (it was short for Mattinson, I think) was a smart, not unpleasant, white-haired lady, and one of those people who managed to be both brisk and vague at the same time. It was to

Mrs Matt that one was sent if feeling ill or requiring any kind of medical attention, and Mrs Matt's diagnosis for just about everything consisted of the word "Mm." Or, if pressed for time, just "M." If you were very lucky you might get an aspirin or maybe a glass of water, but on the rare occasions I ever went to her office by the canteen, I don't remember getting anything at all, except possibly "Mm." My visits – and, with my sick-leave record, this is surprising – probably numbered only two or three in total, and even then one was to accompany someone else. But then, frankly, by the time anyone had inhaled the cooking smells from the adjacent canteen, if they weren't already feeling sick, they soon would be, so probably no one troubled her that often. Strictly speaking, what Mrs Matt actually did was a bit of a mystery.

I once had to dash to the nearest toilet with a classmate who was about to be violently sick. Following the usual "Please, sir..." moment, I hastily headed her towards the open door of the cloakroom opposite our then-form room, Room 14, which happened to be a boys' one, but well, what would you have done? It was either that, or a very long sprint to the girls' toilets, along a corridor and across a yard, and she definitely wasn't going to make it. Sadly, as we emerged, we collided with the senior master who threatened us with the fires of hell. I tried to point out the expediency of the situation, to no avail. Never will I understand Man's lack of logic. This was the same senior master who was particularly offensive to a nice Danish boy in our class who had a slight speech impediment. How he'd have coped with the multiracial society of today, I can't imagine.

Neither of the senior masters, both of whom shall remain nameless, were very attractive characters. Both were fierce and irrational. The first had broken teeth. Apart from his general viciousness, that's about all I can recall of him. After he retired, the second was little better. They had an office opposite our first form room, Room 10, which one tiptoed past very cautiously. Next to us was Room 11, the geography room, where Norman or the other geography teacher, the slightly less entertaining Mr Hickling, could usually be found.

Moving clockwise around the hall, you then came to the headmaster's office, which had a little light over it with an *ENTER* sign which flashed when one was allowed to enter its hallowed portal. That was enough to send a shiver down your spine, for a start. Further round were two classrooms I never remember using at all, then Room 6, which as I recall was the one everyone hated, as the fume cupboard from one of the science labs above was strategically placed above the chimney, so that appalling smells would come down it from time to time, choking those within. Luckily, I never had lessons in there. Then as you left the hall, the next room was Room 7, which was the music room, I'm pretty certain, where poor Miss Rudd kept the Philistines at bay. But there was a certain lack of logic in the room numbering, and I seem to have missed a Room 8 and 9. Maybe they were the ones on the other side of the hall… Since our time there, many of the room numbers have been changed, probably more than once.

On the Room 10 side of the hall was a bust of Herbert Strutt, the founder, and a portrait of the first headmaster, Mr Tunnicliffe, painted in traditional style. I'm not sure by whom, but it was quite impressive. When George Ducker was about to retire, someone decided it would be appropriate if the current art master could be asked to paint his portrait. Since Mr Granger (possibly, with the exception of Dixie, the only memorably baldy) was the sort of artist who liked to throw paint at his canvases and ride over them on a bike, this did not seem to be an awfully good idea. Presumably they offered to pay him, otherwise anything he couldn't actually drill nails into or scatter with gravel or rabbit droppings would have been beneath his contempt, or at least upset his artistic integrity. Not that I ever remember him doing anything that energetic while he was supposed to be teaching us. Mostly he just lounged around being languid. Vaguely, I seem to remember a sort of shocked hush when the portrait was first revealed – I can't remember whether it was officially unveiled in front of us all (maybe I imagined that bit), but it was one of those faintly Chaplinesque moments, when a curtain is whipped aside to reveal something that might best be described as undesirable. There was a sort of ripple of "Oh my God, what's *that*?" followed by a chorus of barely disguised sniggers. Perhaps, to put it kindly, it looked like something a wannabe post-impressionist might have knocked up after a particularly heavy night on the absinthe. Or, to put it less kindly, it was simply god-awful.

Sometime after I'd left school, there was an exhibition of Granger's work in our local art gallery, which is how I found out about his liking for riding a bike over his canvases, and I remember writing something disparaging in the visitors' book. I can't recall exactly what I wrote, but bearing in mind that I was only eighteen or so at the time, I expect it was something fairly puerile. I imagine it had about as much effect on his career as he had on mine.

TWENTY-THREE

The Times They Were A-Changin'...

On looking back, George Ducker, our first headmaster, reminds me slightly of John Le Mesurier, as he appeared in the earlier series of *Dad's Army*, which of course did not appear on our small screens until some ten years later. He was tall, white-haired, distinguished-looking and rather remote, very much the English gentleman. His replacement, R. G. Matthias, by contrast, was stocky, dark-haired, fairly left wing and very Welsh. He was brisk in manner and struck me as being somewhat pugnacious, so it came as quite a surprise to me to discover only recently that he was a pacifist who'd been a conscientious objector during the Second World War. Being only small fry, I never had much to do with either of them, but although distant, both were impressive. Even so, when Mr Ducker held his final school assembly on the last day of the summer term in 1958, most of us shed a tear. Not only was George himself leaving us, but eleven other members of staff were departing also, including Mr West, the maths master, and Mr Quest, who had encouraged my writing in those early years. Perhaps they felt things would not be quite the same again.

R. G. Matthias was deemed rather more progressive than George, and one of the first things he did when he arrived in the autumn of 1958 was change the original Greek names of the forms into common-or-garden English ones, so that our form, which would have been 5 Lower Alpha, became the much less attractive 5 Lower C. This seemed like an immediate step down from our grammar-school status, and we resented it. Probably he was thinking of preparing us for the comprehensive style of education to come, but Strutts had a long-standing academic tradition of which we were proud. In the years to come, schools would become a lot larger, a lot less academic and, in many ways, a lot less efficient, and it's something most of us still heatedly debate.

By the time I'd got into the higher forms, I had discovered it was possible to escape from the dreaded winter games lessons in the Belper mud. I think it was during the last two terms I was there, that I found the sixth form had all their games lessons together, rather than per class, thus making a lot more of us to be counted. It also made it a lot harder for one of us to be missed. So, rather than presenting myself shivering in shorts every Wednesday afternoon, I would sneak furtively upstairs to the welcome, warming fug of the library, looking studious, and find myself a cosy seat in one of the alcoves, where I could sit and watch the mist and freezing fog swirling round the grey, Gothic spike of the clock tower and concealing the Chevin from view. It was lovely. There, in the comforting yellow light of an alcove, I discovered the work of Dylan Thomas – not his poetry, which never

193

particularly grabbed me, but his essays and radio pieces, and most especially his short stories. Since my school report book tended to be scattered with *Could do better*'s and *Must try harder*'s, I doubt my sneaky Wednesday afternoons in the library did me much harm. And it would be another five years or so before that other Dylan, who borrowed his name, made his famous comment that The Times They Were A-Changin'. Yes, they were. For me, and for all of us. But at that stage in my life, I was still hiding in the library every Wednesday and he was probably still plain Mr Zimmerman. And nobody missed me.

It's interesting, on looking back, to read that Dylan Thomas considered his short stories to be potboilers, since as far as I'm concerned, they have way outlived his poetry in terms of their originality and immediacy. While his poetry was more concerned with abstraction, his fiction and essays were very much concerned with the real and the material. But then, Dylan could combine the two so well. I remember reading *Return Journey*, in which he returns to Swansea after the Blitz and visualises the burned-out corridors of his old school, which sounded so like ours, and it really hit me. Many years later, I was to borrow the title for a piece I wrote, which I often read aloud, about a soldier returning in spirit to the battlegrounds of the Spanish Civil War, an event which, because of those disturbing childhood memories, has always been deeply personal for me. Another writer, whose work has sometimes been compared to Dylan's, was to die early in that same war, and was also to influence me in the years to come. His name was Federico García Lorca and he was killed not as a combatant, but merely because he was an artist and a homosexual. It was not until after I left school and had started to learn Spanish at evening classes that I discovered him. But for me then, as now, it was Dylan's prose that grabbed me, with its weird and wonderful use of language that made the ordinary extraordinary, and I sat there in the alcove and read a story called *One Warm Saturday*.

Although the dialogue and the references are dated now, something about that story is just as vivid and just as enthrallingly sordid on looking at it again as it was when I first read it, and even then it was referring to times of twenty years or so earlier. But it grabbed me. It jumped off the page and bit me. It took me with it. Hard to say why, but I suppose, as always with Dylan, it was the language and the way it was used that so impressed me, and the ending in the dilapidated tenement with its wooden floors and creaking stairs, reminding me so much of our warehouse in its final days, surrounded by demolition and devastation, is one of the most vivid pieces of writing I know, and the last, empty, despairing paragraph still blows my mind.

Two other things really hit me around this time. The first was a music appreciation session, led I think by Mr McKay, who had hitherto not been a particular favourite of mine, and the session had only been taken as a choice to fill in a blank space in my timetable. He played a recording of the Broadway production of *West Side Story*, which hit all of us with a hefty wallop. It was certainly pretty robust compared to the more sedate offerings of Miss Rudd. The other was the school production of Thornton Wilder's remarkable play *Our Town* (was Dylan Thomas influenced by this when he wrote *Under Milk Wood*?) – another example of making the ordinary extraordinary – which was so perfectly done that it left everyone who saw it speechless with emotion. (As Wilder said, quoting Molière, "All you need for theatre is a platform and a passion or two.") *Yes*, I thought; *yes!* And although I never considered acting, it was the power of the written word that I felt could be my own way into the arts.

I was much too shy, in fact, to consider acting, although I did – later, after leaving school – join a couple of amateur groups, one of which was highly professional (Gwen Taylor was a former member), and took a couple of walk-on parts in their production of *Milk Wood* myself, but my main interest was watching actors and seeing how plays worked. Strutts had a very high standard of drama productions and a number of pupils went on to become professionals, including a future James Bond and, of course, Alan Bates. But I was far too shy and it wasn't until I started working with actors in the Studio at Derby Playhouse many years later that I began to gain even a small degree of self-confidence. Looking back through my old school reports, I see the comment *She's too quiet*. "Ah, but beware of the quiet ones. They will be taking notes," as I remarked many years later to Norman Robinson.

Many things had changed at home, too, of course, during the six years I was at Strutts. When my parents moved from their three-bedroom semi into their two-bedroom detached bungalow in early 1955, we had no washing machine and no fridge. Washing was done in an electric-powered wash boiler, and squeezed out in a wringer which lived outside in the garage. This was not quite as fearsome as the old-fashioned mangle, but was still operated by hand. There was also a dolly tub out there for large items, which involved squishing stuff around in the bottom of the tub with a plunger-like implement called a ponch, but not often, as sheets and blankets were sent to the laundry which collected and delivered fortnightly. We had a coal fire in the lounge, and in the kitchen a boiler which burned coke and heated our hot water. The bungalow was all electric and had no gas supply, so my mother had to get used to an electric cooker, which she found extremely slow – apart from the grill, which was just the opposite. The smell of burned toast conjures up the spirit of my mother like a genie. It would be unfair to imply that she was a bad cook – she was actually a very good one, but that grill, which took ten minutes to warm up, then incinerated all offerings, was too much. The smell of burned toast returns me instantly to the kitchen at Kingsley Road and my mother hastily wafting a tea towel.

We had no fridge, either, when we first moved there. In fact, few people had, in those days. The large pantry at the semi had been nice and cool, but in the bungalow we had only a small pantry which faced south and got quite hot, so eventually my parents bought a fridge. Prior to this, meat and dairy products etc. had been kept outside in a meat safe, which was a large box a bit like a rabbit hutch, covered with a wire-mesh grille. No doubt the hyperactive ants we inherited would have found their way in there, too, as they did into the pantry, even squeezing their way into a sprinkler bottle of vinegar to drown in the contents.

The kitchen was large and spacious, however, and pleasant enough to eat our meals in if we wanted, and the bungalow boasted a garage, even though at this stage, we had no car. It also had a greenhouse, which had no doubt swayed my mother in its favour, although I think to begin with, like me, she rather regretted leaving the house. She soon established tomato plants and chrysanthemums in there, and the smells of these also remind me of her. My favourite photograph of my parents shows them in the greenhouse together, with Mum's precious chrysanths. The garden was well stocked with fruit – two different kinds of apple trees, gooseberries, blackcurrants and raspberry canes, which were very prolific. There was also a tall pear tree, equally prolific, but bearing particularly tasteless pears which nobody would eat except the dog. Peggy used to jump up and grab them, but even she tired of their watery mushiness after a while, and Dad cut the tree down and planted beans where it had grown. It also made more room for my railway-sleeper swing, which had come with us. The new garden was more private than our previous one, which again went in its favour. The only neighbour visible from the garden was Mr Brown, the kindly, elderly Aberdonian, whose TV I sometimes went to watch and who soon became a family friend. The bungalow itself, however, was a lot less private, or so I felt, with its bedrooms at the front and, worse still, the toilet exactly opposite the front door, so that should anyone call while you were enthroned, so to speak, they knew exactly where you were; deeply embarrassing, should the door blow open at an inappropriate moment.

There were the remains of an air-raid shelter in the garden, but only a slab of roof and a projecting metal chimney were still visible, the rest having presumably been filled in. Despite this rather gloomy memento of a war I didn't actually remember, I was slightly sorry I couldn't get inside it to see what it would have been like. People were still not talking about the War, though its shadow remained, fainter now, but giving us a reminder every now and then. At the back of the house were still open fields, though shortly they too would be built on. The air of impermanence was fading.

Our old friends on the other side moved away after a year or two, and their slightly creepy bungalow was occupied by a number of families in rapid succession, which on reflection was perhaps suspect, but it had been bought by an army couple (Normanton Barracks was still in operation at this time) who let it to other army folk who came and went for some years before it was sold again. However, I never heard any stories of strange, skeletal figures appearing in bedrooms. Perhaps the presence of military personnel put off any spectral visitors. Even so, I was never comfortable in that house, no matter who lived there. According to my cousin, a line of geophysical stress does indeed go right under it, and progresses down and over the road and under the house where the Fallen Madonna of dirty phone calls lived (and again, shortly moved away, to my relief), but misses both the houses we lived in. Thank goodness for that. Maybe I wasn't imagining things after all.

TWENTY-FOUR

Into the '60s

It was already 1960 by the time I took my GCEs, known simply then as O Levels. To my (and perhaps everyone's) amazement, I passed six out of seven, failing only maths. (No surprise there, then.) The Scripture paper, which many of us had opted to take, little heathens that we were, as it was always reckoned to be a doddle, turned out not to be, and I only just scraped through, but it was still a pass, nonetheless, and a lot of others didn't. We were lucky with our English set books, being *The Merchant of Venice*, which we'd done before, Wordsworth (not difficult), and H. G. Wells' *The History of Mr Polly* (a walkover). I gained a distinction in art, probably thanks to Miss Asher who had been teaching us in those final terms. I was awarded the Arts Prize for the year.

Sandra, who had also done well, had left at the end of summer term to take up a clerical job at a local factory, but I decided to stay on and have a try at A Levels since my previous results had been promising. I opted to do English,

French and geography, but not art, as I knew I would have to study with Mr Granger and couldn't bear the thought. Also, my parents didn't feel that art alone would offer many career opportunities at the time. At this stage, I had no idea what I wanted to do after school anyway, though I would have liked to pursue my interest in languages. It turned out to be an unfortunate choice, since at the end of the first term, or maybe halfway through it, the English teacher with whom we'd been studying Chaucer fell ill, and we were fobbed off with several temporary teachers or none at all. Miss Saull, the formidable French mistress, ignored me completely, and only half of our geography lessons were with Norman, the others being with another teacher whom I found singularly uninspiring.

The only saving grace was Shakespeare with Miss Simister, also formidable but, at the same time, pretty inspirational. Although apt to be scary, she certainly knew how to bring the Bard to life. Sitting on a high stool with her gown and skirts hitched and revealing her nether garments to the unfortunates on the front row (I'm sure they would have been highly respectable Directoires), she would spiel forth at length on the glories of his work with wild enthusiasm. "A very *spacious* play," she exclaimed regarding *Antony and Cleopatra*, and on re-reading it, I do see exactly what she meant. It does expound an awful lot of wide-ranging grandeur, not to say unbridled passion. *Let Rome in Tiber melt, and the wide arch of the ranged empire fall...* etc. – and why not, indeed?

I still have fond memories, though, of what should have been a very moving moment towards the final tragedy, when a doomed Cleopatra envisages herself mocked as a circus act, paraded through the streets of Rome in the guise of some squeaking boy, *I' the posture of a whore*. Sadly the poor lad engaged to read this line was unacquainted with the word, which he pronounced 'woo-er', causing Miss S to respond, in best back-of-the-stalls voice, "The word, Clibury, is pronounced '*hore*' and it means *a common prostitute*." I've spared him further embarrassment by editing his name slightly, but he went an unflattering shade of pink, to the accompaniment of much tittering. Can anything be more deadening to the work of any writer than hearing it read out loud by kids (or indeed, anyone) who can't act? Or pronounce words like 'whore'. Ah, titter ye not; probably half of us didn't know what it meant either. I think *Ant and Cleo* is probably my favourite of the Shakespeares that we studied. I do have another fond memory of someone during a performance murmuring, during one of Cleo's rapturous soliloquies, "She does go on a bit, doesn't she?" (My husband, probably.) True, but she does it awfully well. I think if I had to plump for one to sit through, though, it would have to be *The Tempest*, which I love, probably because it is a) weird, and b) short. I know, I know, but I do get numb round the bum nowadays...

Autumn term 1960 began bright and sunny, but I missed Sandra, and although some old friends were still there, life was not quite the same, somehow. Eileen was around, but doing different subjects, and as always, much to my annoyance, at the end of the summer term, all the tennis nets had been taken down and the dreaded hockey sessions began again, despite the fact that the sun was still shining and the weather was warm. Eileen, her friend Pauline, Holly (who believed the world was going to end in 1963 and was sadly disappointed) and I still gathered at lunchtime on the bank of the playing fields opposite the Chevin, eyeing the local talent on the football pitch and chatting.

Of course, many of the boys we were keen on, being older than us, had left, which rather took the shine off things. On the other hand, being in the sixth form ourselves now, we were obliged to feel slightly more important. By the time the bad weather came, the library beckoned, and most hockey lessons were evaded within its welcoming walls. Strangely enough, on my last school report, someone (Bandy's replacement, a Miss Wright, I presume) had written, *Fairly good progress made in hockey this term*. Perhaps she was confusing me with someone else.

There was only one boy at school who ever showed much interest in me, and sad to say, I was rotten to him. I think it was probably because he was slightly younger than I was, and also because I thought initially, in disbelief, he was just being daft. By the time we'd got into the sixth form, he had been put into the same year, but by this time, not surprisingly, he'd lost interest. I can't blame him, really. In retrospect, sorry!

I think romance in school had been killed off for me by those early days of dragging round the gym in plimsolls pretending to do country dancing (and I do mean dragging) with some unfortunate that I couldn't stand, and vice versa. Possibly the plimsoll is the most unromantic item of footwear ever dreamed up by a shoemaker, and furthermore, they always smelled unenticingly of rubber and stuck to the floor. And so did we. Not being deemed particularly attractive, unlike Eileen, I never had a queue of prospective suitors chafing at the bit. On the other hand, they probably didn't know she kept a little red book in which she noted down their qualities and performance scores. When I unwisely mentioned this at a reunion some forty years later, a couple of them paled considerably and headed at speed towards the nearest little boys' room. I'm not quite sure what for, since by that time, Eileen had long since emigrated, and their intimate details were doubtless well and truly forgotten. Ah, the follies of youth...

In the early summer of 1960, my cousin Tessa married her Greek Cypriot doctor, and there is a photo of me with the group outside Uncle Ben's house in Harewood Road, Allestree, with George, the new husband, looking so remarkably like my uncle (Tessa's father) in *his* wedding photograph that they could well have been the same person. Sadly, the marriage turned out to be almost as disastrous. Tessa had made her own dress, and typically for Tess, I do seem to recall noticing a few tacking stitches still in it. I'm wearing my tartan dress, of which I was fond, and another photo shows me with Gran standing outside Allestree Church. Gran would have been almost eighty. Tessa was twenty-four and I would have been sixteen. Gran died almost exactly a year later. Tessa, by then, may well have been in Cyprus where she lived for a number of years, returning there to live with his family for a while after she had separated from George. The rest of her life was spent mainly in Leeds, where she died in 1987. By this time, we had not met for fifteen years, but even now, I often think of her.

I can't recall a great deal more about the summer of 1960. I imagine a lot of it was spent waiting for the dreaded O Level results, which, luckily for me, turned out well. The '60s, as such, didn't really begin to swing until around 1963. I remember being told by Jean, my childhood friend from Darley Abbey, whose family had moved to Buckinghamshire by this time, about this fabulous new group called The Beatles. "Spelled with an 'a'," she added, for further clarification.

"Oh, yeah?" I replied, with little enthusiasm. Who? I'd never heard of them. That first single that made the world sit up wasn't released until 1962, so maybe it was the year after I'd left school that she made this remark. However, I must have visited them in Chesham around the late summer of 1960, as there is a photo of me there, with my newly grown hair (still short, though, at Tessa's wedding) tied back in a ponytail. I recall Auntie A (of exotic trifle fame) showing off a bit about the wonders of Bucks and feeling sorry for anyone who didn't live there, although of course it had been beautiful at their previous home in Doncaster, also.

"No it wasn't," muttered Jean. "There was a great big slag heap at the bottom of the garden!"

Until then, the only group I liked even slightly seemed to have been The Everly Brothers. Buddy Holly was okay, if a bit annoying, but he had pace. Elvis left me cold. Skiffle was fashionable in my early days at Strutts and we even had a skiffle band, complete with washboards and tea chest (did it really have a pair of old braces stretched over it? I can't remember!), but that was just a bit of fun. The first Beatles songs I genuinely liked were 'Michelle' and 'Yesterday', both a bit on the sad side, but utterly different from anything in the line of pop music we'd heard before. Even my mother was impressed. But in 1960, the Beatles were probably still faffing around wondering whether or not to continue their education, just like us...

Our set novel for the autumn term of 1960 was *Sons and Lovers*, which came as something of a delightful surprise to us all, for several reasons; firstly because it was local, and also because *Lady Chatterley's Lover* had only just been taken off the banned books list as being considered suitable for 'one's wife or servants to read', so naturally, reading anything by Lawrence was considered a great adventure. I empathised with Paul Morel immediately (apart from, as with all women, I imagine, his ultimate unkind treatment of Miriam), and was particularly caught by his comment in the early part of the book, when leaving Nottingham Station with his mother. He looks over the bridge onto the canal between the high factory walls and says, *"It's just like Venice."* It amused me, because as a child, I had often looked over the same bridge and thought exactly the same thing!

Autumn term was made memorable by the arrival of a group of American students from Indiana whose parents were working on a contract with Rolls-Royce for a while. These included the Nelson twins, Maren and Karen, from Indianapolis, who were in the same class as me, and I am still in touch with them all these years later. Together with their younger brother Brian, there were around nine of them altogether, and I last met them when they came over on a visit in the 1990s. Among their memories are being traumatised by hockey in the Belper mud and being dissuaded from swinging their hockey sticks like golf clubs, and the freezing temperature of our classrooms, which Maren said tended to echo a bit. She didn't mention that you could sometimes see your breath, as well. Due to the echo, she said she had to listen very carefully to what the teachers were saying until she got used to the accent.

Considering that the teachers would have been among the better-spoken folk around, I'm wondering how they coped with the locals, since Belper people, perhaps due to their French inheritance, tend to speak very quickly (or, to put it as my mother did, they 'clack', a good French word to describe it). Despite having so many French surnames in the town to this day, from both Norman times and from the Huguenot textile workers who came later, most of our pupils were crap at French, but maybe that was due to being bullied by Miss Saull. Belperites also speak loudly, probably due to an inborn need to yell over the noise of textile machinery, and even though most of the mills have now gone, anyone travelling from Belper to Derby by bus, as I sometimes do, is likely to be deaf by the time they reach the end of their journey. And although the millworkers' cottages are often tarted up and marketed as des res dwellings nowadays, which makes me laugh, and the shops are rather posher than they used to be, they still say, "'Ello, duck" when you go in, and the town's still the same as it ever was; a bit rough and ready but with its heart in the right place. I'll always have a soft spot for it.

Maren and Karen both have very fond memories of their time at Strutts. They remember our trip to the Royal Shakespeare Company at Stratford and having fish and chips on the coach on the way home, after we'd waited ages for the driver and a couple of the lads to emerge from the nearest pub – I can't imagine that going down very well with Health and Safety nowadays. They also remembered the school Christmas carol service at St Peter's Church, higher up the town, since the school had long outgrown its capacity for seating visitors, and indeed, most of us, in the hall. For similar reasons, Founders Day (or Speech Day, as it was usually known) was usually held elsewhere, and I have a particularly fond memory of one of the Nonconformist chapels in Bridge Street, where a large lump of plaster fell off the ceiling and exploded like a silent bomb onto the audience below, to the great delight of those of us sitting on the balcony. It enlivened the tedium no end.

Strangely enough, I can't remember my last day at Strutts at all. Because I left at Easter 1961 instead of the end of the summer term, there weren't any farewell speeches or anything like that. No tears, no tantrums. My parents had spotted a job in the library service that looked suitable, I applied for it and got it, and that was that. I can't say I really regretted it, although I later wished I had been able to go to university, but at that time, places were few, and it was also necessary to pass maths, which would have been an impossibility. I had no great desire to teach, so teacher training college was out of the question.

I finally got to university at the tender age of forty-seven. In the meantime, I'd attended what was then the Derby College of Art and Technology, now the University of Derby, to study librarianship on day release (and very boring it was, too), and passed a number of exams, done courses in art, theatre studies,

Spanish and geology, and written a dozen plays, three of which had full professional productions. Three other plays had student productions, one broadcast, and a TV play, my first, was commissioned though never went into production, as well as some short plays for women which had well-received public readings, so I hadn't done too badly. I'd also married and had three children, all of whom did get to university, and my husband had more letters after his name than there were in it. By the time I'd gained a 2.1 in photography at the University of Derby, I was fifty. I took the academic route, involving a dissertation on personal history seen through family photographs, which gained a first. While I wouldn't say we were a madly academic family, we all worked extremely hard for what we achieved.

I loved my time at Strutts and was proud to have been a pupil there. If I have any regrets about my time at school (and indeed, later), it would be that there were people who could have helped me, and at very little cost to themselves, who simply chose not to. To those who did help, at school, in the theatre and elsewhere, I'm immensely grateful. It always seems to me that if people were encouraged to excel at the things they are good at, rather than trying to achieve a modicum of mediocrity in what others deem to be more important, a lot less talent would be wasted and a lot more people would be happy. But what I wanted most of all was the freedom to be accepted for what I was and what I could do, without prejudice or petty, mindless criticism. Was that a lot to ask? I had my fifteen minutes of fame, and maybe if I'd packed my bags and gone off to London to risk ending up living in a cardboard box under a bridge somewhere, they might have lasted a bit longer, but my roots are here in Derbyshire, the place I love, and that's good enough for me.

TWENTY-FIVE

Home Ground

I suppose you might say that both sides of my family, in their
ancestral migrations, were heavily influenced by the presence
of the River Trent. My mother's paternal grandfather
came on foot as a poor young man in search of work, sleeping
in ditches, surviving as he could in a bitter winter, from the
flatlands of Lincolnshire towards Nottingham and eventually
Derby, where he settled and married a local girl. My mother's
maternal grandfather's people came from the very south of
Staffordshire, in an area now part of Shropshire, up the valley
of the Trent to Barton-under-Needwood and Walton-on-Trent,
stopping for a few years on the edge of the Black Country. His
wife's family came from the Staffordshire-Derbyshire border,
close to the Potteries, as did most of my father's folk, who
migrated towards Burton and Derby with the building of the
railway. The rest, I think, were Derby born and bred, as am I.

The Trent is England's second-longest river and arguably
its most treacherous. Benign and beguiling, devious and

dangerous, and totally lacking any sense of direction whatever, it swings and swerves from one side of the country to the other, up, down and sideways, determined to go wherever it wants at any cost, as anyone who gets in its way is sure to find out. Yes, if the Trent was a person, it would definitely be a politician.

It used to be said that it is the Trent that divides the North of England from the Midlands, but of course, geographically, this simply doesn't make sense. Nothing that changes direction that often could actually divide anything, except possibly opinion. It does slice places like Nottingham and Burton straight through the middle, however, leaving them with a bit of a problem, especially when it floods. Which is often. Not for nothing does its name mean 'The Trespasser'. On the credit side, when this happens, at least if you don't happen to be standing in the way, it can look very beautiful. The Trent misses Derby altogether – presumably it has better things to do – but of course, my home town has its tributary, the Derwent, swift, sinuous and equally moody, which so happily flooded our school playing fields in Belper, a few miles further north. This fact, of course, made the line in our school song – *Where the Derwent flows by the Chevin on its far way to the sea* – geographically incorrect (did Norman Robinson ever point this out to Mr Sutton, the senior history master, who wrote it?), but it's a lovely song, anyway, so no one seemed to mind. And when the Derwent flooded and froze in winter and stopped us having to play hockey, I didn't mind at all.

People tend to think of Derbyshire only as the Peak District, but of course, that's only part of it. South Derbyshire, East and Central Derbyshire (which, with the Nottinghamshire border, D. H. Lawrence called "The country of my heart"), and the Trent Valley are not the Peak District at all. But they are the heart of England. That beating heart of England, between Charnwood on the horizon and the Chevin, is my own personal space, and I claim the latter is where the North begins. One day, as we were driving along the A6 towards Belper, as we crossed over the Derwent at Milford at the foot of the Chevin, where the road makes an abrupt ninety-degree turn, one of my daughters, who was about ten at the time, remarked, quite out of the blue, "Everything changes here." And suddenly, I saw what she meant. On one side of the river were hedges and fences and buildings largely of brick, and on the far side, the fields were divided by stone walls and the buildings, too, were of stone. She was absolutely right, of course. I had travelled that road every day for six years and never thought about it before. As you take that turn across the Derwent and head north alongside the long green slope of the Chevin, the last hill in the Pennines, you are in stone-wall country. So there you have it. The North of England begins at Milford. I have it on good authority.

The Chevin lies alongside the Derwent like some large, friendly animal, a purring cat, perhaps, basking in the sunshine. It gives the impression that it's very happy to be there. And that was how it appeared from the windows and playgrounds of our school. In winter, it shivered a bit, but it was still docile enough, at least, to those of us down below. Turn south again along the A6, and climb on foot to the top of Bunkers Hill on the way to Quarndon, that curious elevated spot that doesn't look high at all, where once I heard the hummadruz one summer afternoon many years ago, and thought I saw the house that wasn't there. Look south and slightly west as far as you can see, and there is Charnwood Forest, the oldest and most enigmatic piece of land in England, a few blue humps on the horizon. Look over a surprising panorama across the valley of the Trent in wonder, for there they lie, as they have for almost seven hundred million years: the bare and ancient hills of Charnwood, rising still, as they did above the ice sheets, islands once in a coral sea, sleeping dogs across the threshold of history.

About the Author

Brenda Ray was born in Derby in 1944. She was educated at the Herbert Strutt Grammar School in Belper and at the University of Derby. She has worked in librarianship and as a creative writing tutor, and in the 1980s, as a freelance playwright. Her first stage play, REHEARSAL, a drama about the Spanish Civil War, was produced at Derby Playhouse Studio in 1980, followed by a Wild West comedy with music, STICK 'EM UP! in 1984, and later a black comedy, DRESSING UP, about suburban women under the threat of violence, at Croydon Warehouse in 1985, with other productions at smaller venues. When professional theatre opportunities began to dry up, due to arts and education cuts, she returned to college in the 1990s and gained a BA Hons. in Photography at the University of Derby. She later returned to librarianship, as a part time librarian for a law firm, and returned to her first love, short story writing, publishing her collection, THE SIREN OF SALAMANCA, in 2008. The title story won the Cornhill Allianz Short Story Prize at the Guildford Book Festival in 2005. Then followed a second collection, GONDWANALAND, in 2013. The title story was awarded a prize in the HE Bates Short Story Competition in 2011.

Brenda Ray lives in Derby and has three daughters and three grandchildren. BETWEEN CHARNWOOD AND THE CHEVIN is her first work of non-fiction.